TOUGHING IT OUT
IN AFGHANISTAN

To Judy and Bill
Korstad

with Light

regards

Mike
Ottaton

The exterior of Qala Ikhtyarudin in Herat, Afghanistan.

TOUGHING IT OUT IN AFGHANISTAN

Michael E. O'Hanlon
Hassina Sherjan

BROOKINGS INSTITUTION PRESS
Washington, D.C.

Library of Congress Cataloging-in-Publication data

O'Hanlon, Michael E.
  Toughing it out in Afghanistan / Michael O'Hanlon, Hassina Sherjan.
    p.   cm.
  Includes bibliographical references and index.
  ISBN 978-0-8157-0409-6 (pbk. : alk. paper)
  1. Afghan War, 2001– 2. Afghanistan—Strategic aspects. 3. United States—
Military policy. 4. Counterinsurgency—Afghanistan. 5. Taliban. I. Sherjan,
Hassina. II. Title.

  DS371.412.O37 2010
  958.104'7—dc22   2009050451

9 8 7 6 5 4 3 2 1

Printed on acid-free paper

Typeset in Sabon

Composition by Cynthia Stock
Silver Spring, Maryland

Printed by R. R. Donnelley
Harrisonburg, Virginia

To the brave people of Afghanistan
and their many friends around the world

The Middle East and Asia

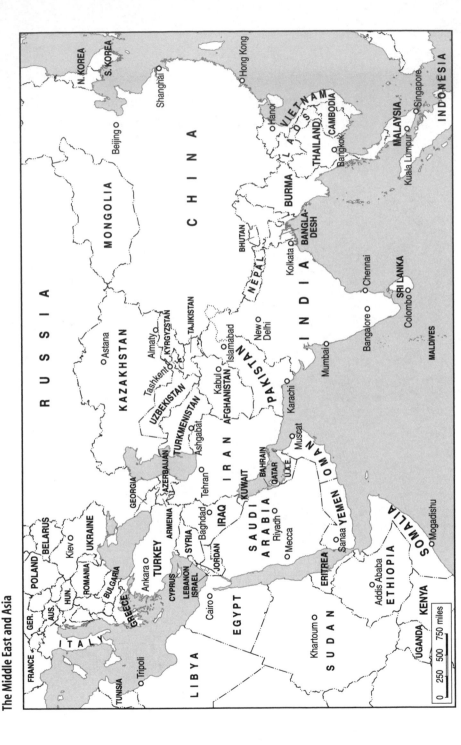

Contents

List of Maps

Foreword

At first glance Afghanistan does not seem to be a place of any importance to Americans. Afghanistan is a remote and land-locked country of mountains and deserts on the far side of the planet from North America. It is desperately poor. Its only significant export is drugs made from the poppy plants that grow in its valleys. For three decades it has been wracked by foreign invasion, civil war, and terror. Millions of Afghans have died or been displaced in these wars.

But two of the most significant events of our times had their origins in Afghanistan. The first was the defeat of the Soviet Union's Fortieth Red Army in the 1980s, a defeat that signaled the collapse of the Union of Soviet Socialist Republics and the end of the cold war. The second was the attack on September 11, 2001, by al Qaeda, which was planned and orchestrated from Afghan territory. While tens of millions of Americans watched in horror the collapse of the twin towers, Osama bin Laden and Mullah Omar—the leaders of al Qaeda and its ally the Taliban—watched with joy in Kandahar.

Now Afghanistan is the battlefield in America's longest war. The defeat of the Russian army in 1989 was followed by an American abandonment of Afghanistan that led to the rise of the Taliban and al Qaeda. The attacks of 9/11 led to the American invasion and the start of the current war. The tragedy is that it need not have been a long war. Had the United States put the resources into stabilizing Afghanistan in 2002,

2003, and 2004 after it had liberated the country from al Qaeda and the Taliban, the war would probably be over by now. Today we cannot go back and fix those mistakes, but we must deal with the consequences of them.

Despite appearances, Afghanistan is a country that matters a great deal to Americans and to the international community. We now know that the consequences of ignoring what happens in Kandahar, Herat, and Kabul can be deadly in New York, Madrid, and London. We have also learned that Afghan developments have enormous impact on its neighbor Pakistan and throughout south and central Asia. The revival of the Taliban in Afghanistan has now spread across the Durand Line into Pakistan, where it threatens to destabilize a nuclear weapons state.

Fortunately, we are not alone in Afghanistan. The North Atlantic Treaty Organization took on the Afghan mission in 2003, and thousands of European and Canadian soldiers are now fighting alongside our troops and the Afghan National Army. Soldiers from other allies, including Australia, Sweden, and the United Arab Emirates, have also joined the effort.

The question we all confront today is: Can we still succeed in Afghanistan despite the mistakes of the past? This book addresses that central issue at the critical time. *Toughing It Out in Afghanistan* crisply and eloquently makes the argument that it is not yet too late but that the window of time to win is not large. It makes the case that if we act resolutely and resource the effort properly, we can still succeed in building a better future in Afghanistan.

It is fitting that this book is a collaborative effort of an American and an Afghan because we cannot succeed in Afghanistan without a partnership with each other. There is no made-in-America solution to the challenges we face today in Afghanistan or Pakistan. Just as American support was crucial to the mujahedin's victory over the Soviets, so too is American support today crucial to helping Afghans and Pakistanis defeat the terrorists who threaten their freedoms. But now Afghans and Pakistanis must in the end bear the lion's share of the challenge today, just as they did in defeating communism thirty years ago.

In his first month in office, President Barack Hussein Obama invited Afghanistan and Pakistan to send teams of their top officials to Washington to help America review its policy toward their countries. I chaired those meetings in the restored and elegant office of the Secretary of War in the Eisenhower Executive Office Building. As we discussed what to do in this conflict with our partners, I came to respect deeply their courage in persevering. As they say, they are fighting for their children's futures against a cruel and evil foe.

Our children's future is also at stake in Afghanistan and Pakistan. A jihadist victory in Afghanistan against NATO would be as much a global game changer as was the defeat of the Fortieth Red Army. With a secure base in South Asia, the global jihadists would threaten us as never before. Our most important alliance, NATO, would be shattered. So we must find the way to succeed. This book offers a timely blueprint for how to do so.

BRUCE RIEDEL
The Brookings Institution

Acknowledgments

The authors are grateful to many colleagues and friends, including members of the Afghanistan government, the international military presence, or ISAF, the international diplomatic community in Kabul, and government officials as well as think tank colleagues in Washington, Ottawa, and Oslo. They are particularly indebted to Vanda Felbab-Brown, David Gordon, Martin Indyk, Fred Kagan, and Bruce Riedel, who read drafts of the book, and to Jason Campbell, Ian Livingston, Heather Messera, Johanna Peet, and Jeremy Shapiro, as well as Gail Chalef, who did so much with the Afghanistan Index over the last two years.

The authors also thank the team at the Brookings Press, including Larry Converse, Robert Faherty, Chris Kelaher, Janet Walker, and Susan Woollen. In addition, we would like to acknowledge the Perry/Castaneda Library Map Collection, at the University of Texas–Austin, for its useful collection of maps used as a starting point for the maps included here.

TOUGHING IT OUT IN AFGHANISTAN

Afghan Provinces and Major Cities

Map of Afghanistan and surrounding countries showing provinces and major cities.

CHINA

TAJIKISTAN

Northern Areas

INDIA

KASHMIR

o Srinagar

o Jammu

o Amritsar

Ludhiana o

AZAD KASHMIR

Lahore o

PAKISTAN

NORTHWEST FRONTIER PROV.

Peshawar o

Islamabad ⊙

◉ Capital

o Major city/province capital in Afghanistan

100 Miles

0

DUSHANBE ◉

Faizabad o

o Taloqan

TAKHAR BADAKHSHAN

Parun o

NURISTAN

A. o

KUNAR

J.

Pul-e Khumri o

Kunduz o

KUNDUZ

PANJSHIR

B.

M.

K.

Charikar o

PARWAN

M.

Kabul ◉

LA.

KA.

M.J.

NANGARHAR

KHOST

K.o

Gardez o

PAKTIYA

Sharan o

PAKTIKA

Aibak o

SAMANGAN

BAGHLAN

Maidan Shahr o

WARDAK

LO.

P.

Ghazni o

GHAZNI

Termiz

BALKH

Mazar-e Sharif o

Bamyan o

BAMYAN

UZBEK-ISTAN

Sar-e Pul o

SAR-E PUL

JOWZJAN

Shibirghan o

Nili o

DAYKUNDI

Chaghcharan o

GHOR

URUZGAN

Tarin Kot o

ZABUL

Qalat o

Kandahar o

KANDAHAR

Quetta o

BALOCHISTAN

Maimanah o

FARYAB

Qal'ah-ye Now o

BADGHIS

AFGHANISTAN

Mary o

Herat o

HERAT

FARAH

Farah o

Lashkar Gah o

HELMAND

Zaranj o

NIMROZ

TURKMENISTAN

IRAN

IRAN

Provinces
K.   Kapisa
KA. Kabul
LA. Laghman
LO. Logar

Abbreviations
Cities
A. Asadabad
B. Bazarak
J. Jalalabad
K. Khost
M. Mahmud-e Raqi
P. Pul-e 'Alam

CHAPTER ONE

Introduction

"Make no mistake: we do not want to keep our troops in Afghanistan. We seek no military bases there. It is agonizing for America to lose our young men and women. It is costly and politically difficult to continue this conflict. We would gladly bring every single one of our troops home if we could be confident that there were not violent extremists in Afghanistan and Pakistan determined to kill as many Americans as they possibly can."

—President Barack Obama, June 4, 2009[1]

"Conditions on the ground are now much more difficult than in 2002 when the Afghan people overwhelmingly welcomed the international intervention. The goals set, however, are still achievable if the needs and aspirations of the Afghan people are the focus of renewed efforts."

—Former Afghanistan finance minister Ashraf Ghani, April 2009[2]

Afghanistan has become America's longest war. Eight years after the United States set out to destroy the al Qaeda terrorist network responsible for the September 11 attacks on New York and Washington, along with the Taliban regime that gave it sanctuary, American and NATO troops were still in Afghanistan fighting a resurgent Taliban in a war that had not achieved its original objectives and that threatened to have negative effects on the stability of neighboring Pakistan. Barack Obama promised during his presidential campaign that he would refocus on Afghanistan, that the previous administration had made a mistake by turning away from it. But the Obama administration's decisions in March and then December 2009 to increase America's commitment to the country have raised questions about how many American lives and how much of its wealth should be spent on the effort.

Secretary of Defense Robert M. Gates, in a CBS interview in early 2009, lamented that the mission in Afghanistan, like any war, is extremely painful for those actually carrying it out. Since 2008 Afghanistan has, on average, been a more dangerous place for American soldiers to deploy than Iraq. Costs are high not only for the families of those who have died in battle, but also for those physically wounded, those afflicted with psychological trauma, and those who have been deployed time and time again in recent years.

For many years the Afghanistan war was fought with minimal effort. U.S. troop commitments were typically one-tenth as large as those for Iraq during President George W. Bush's first term; NATO allies contributed too, but their troop numbers were even more modest than America's during most of the effort. NATO sought to build an Afghan security force less than one-fifth the size of Iraq's, even though Afghanistan is larger and slightly more populous than Iraq. And it did not provide the necessary trainers to help that smaller force; in early 2009, for example, only one-fourth of all police units had embedded mentors from international partners like the United States.[3]

This situation has changed. Combined foreign forces, organized under a NATO-led mission, numbered more than 100,000 at the end of 2009 and headed to 140,000 in 2010. With annual U.S. costs reaching about $100 billion, it is hardly cheap in financial terms either.

The war is also Afghanistan's longest. It is essentially a conflict that goes back thirty years, to the Soviet invasion. Modern Afghanistan is about as old as the United States, and over the last two and a half centuries, it has never seen such a protracted period of conflict. Britain and Russia played out their "great game" of geostrategic competition at Afghanistan's expense throughout much of the nineteenth century, but this was not a period of continued fighting as the last thirty years have been.

Is the war in Afghanistan now a quagmire? Can the United States and its allies still "win?" Can Afghans really come together as a country to unify their land and build a modern state? Are the stakes really worth it for the United States as well as for other Western powers fighting in this part of the world? Finally, how will we know if the strategy is succeeding as intended?

These are questions increasingly being asked by the American people and Congress. The skeptics include many members of President Obama's own Democratic party, such as Representative David Obey, who has warned Mr. Obama that his Afghanistan-Pakistan strategy has the potential to "devour" his presidency. Vice President Joe Biden is also reported to be wary of a counterinsurgency strategy requiring large numbers of American forces.[4] These are also the questions addressed by this short book. It is designed to help readers understand more about Afghanistan and the war there. It is meant to help inform the American and broader international debate on Afghanistan in 2010 and 2011—absolutely crucial years. As the 2010 fighting season unfolds, we expect another tough and bloody period of combat. The Afghanistan "surge" is not producing results as fast as the Iraq surge did in 2007, and citizens around the world have a right to know why. They also deserve to know how much longer they must be patient, how much longer they must tolerate the high costs in lives and treasure, before a turnaround can reasonably be expected.

At this point, in early 2010, we strongly support the war effort. That is perhaps no surprise. One of us is an Afghan American living in Kabul and trying to help rebuild her country. The other is a defense scholar who became a major supporter of the surge in Iraq and believes strongly in military strategies for counterinsurgency that emphasize protection of the indigenous population and development of local institutions. (He is also a former Peace Corps volunteer in Congo who has seen the consequences of international disinterest and disengagement in a conflict-prone country.) The new Obama strategy for Afghanistan has these basic emphases as well. But as analysts, we know that no war effort should be sustained indefinitely if it fails to achieve progress. In addition to making the case for the current Afghan-NATO strategy, therefore, we also try to project how long it should be before a major improvement in conditions is plainly visible. And we have numerous suggestions, on the military and civilian sides, for how the strategy can be improved.

Perhaps the idea of winning is wrong-headed; winning implies a definitive end, whereas extremism in Afghanistan has been around for decades and may not be within our power to eliminate. But we do think that by 2011, this war can turn around and that by 2013 or so—when the U.S. and NATO role in the war will reach the twelve-year mark—there will be a chance to turn over the main effort to Afghans themselves. True success may take some additional time; building a strong Afghan state and strong economy after so many years of conflict will likely take a generation. But making Afghanistan strong enough to continue the war-fighting and state-building effort itself, while depriving al Qaeda and the Taliban of sanctuaries within Afghanistan from which to attack other countries, is quite likely achievable within a few years. Now that the effort is to be properly resourced with the additional troops that the war's commander, General Stanley A. McChrystal, has requested and the additional civilian support and aid money Ambassador Karl Eikenberry has asked for, we believe that if the Afghan government can make at least some strides toward greater reform and greater effectiveness on the ground for its people, the odds of at least partial success are good—certainly better than 50 percent.

THE STAKES

Just how important is this war, anyway? This is a fair question as the nation doubles down its bets and commits more of its sons and daughters than ever before to a faraway conflict in a remote part of the world.

The simplest answer to this question is to prevent another 9/11 that might originate on Afghan soil, as the original September 11, 2001, attack did. All nineteen hijackers trained there, as have many other anti-Western terrorists over the years. The leadership of al Qaeda and associated movements has now pledged loyalty to Mullah Omar, head of the Afghanistan Taliban, and al Qaeda has trained the Taliban in various methods of attack. Intelligence reports also suggest growing ties between al Qaeda and another major insurgent militia with an extremist ideology, the so-called Haqqani network operating in Afghanistan's east (especially in Khost, Paktia, and Paktika provinces).[5] So the triumph of insurgent groups in Afghanistan would likely lead to a renewed home and sanctuary for al Qaeda within Afghanistan, with a friendly government protecting it—greatly facilitating its training, coordination, and command-and-control efforts globally. Such a sanctuary would be very troubling. Some say it would matter little, given al Qaeda's various other options for organizing its followers. However, the degree of brainwashing required of people being trained to be suicide bombers in the pursuit of a perverted version of jihad is extreme. The notion that it can happen on a large scale just anywhere or through the Internet is improbable; that is not the way extremist movements tend to develop devout followers.[6]

As Gordon Smith, a Canadian official and scholar, plainly put it, in words that would apply equally well to most Western countries including the United States: "It is in Canada's interest that Afghanistan and the bordering regions of Pakistan not again be used as a base from which global terrorist attacks can be launched: think of London, Madrid, Bali and Mumbai, as well as 9/11."[7] As bad as the first few incidents on Smith's list were themselves, 9/11 was far worse—and 9/11 was the plot that benefited in large measure from al Qaeda's ability to organize on Afghan soil.

The stakes, however, go beyond simply denying al Qaeda another sanctuary. Afghanistan has special importance in the minds of al Qaeda—and would-be recruits of al Qaeda—as a symbol of a successful attack against the West. Were we to lose there, al Qaeda would argue that its predictions about the West's weakness and lack of staying power were correct. It would claim momentum in its broader, global struggle against "infidels." That could help the terrorists find new followers who wanted to be on the winning side of history. It would also restore momentum to al Qaeda, momentum that it has lost across the globe from Iraq to Saudi Arabia to Indonesia and elsewhere. The head of the British armed forces, General Sir David Richards, stated that a NATO "failure [in Afghanistan] would have a catalytic effect on militant Islam around the world and in the region because the message would be that al-Qaeda and the Taliban have defeated the US and the British and NATO, the most powerful alliance in the world. So why wouldn't that have an intoxicating effect on militants everywhere? The geo-strategic implications would be immense."[8]

Some say that the Taliban and other Afghan resistance movements are not our real enemies and that we should reach an accommodation with them. But many with firsthand experience of the Taliban in recent years would beg to differ. David Rohde of the *New York Times,* who was held captive in late 2008 and much of 2009 by the group, vividly described the extreme degrees of hatred for the United States, and support for al Qaeda's global agenda, among its members. As counterterrorism expert Bruce Riedel says, "Terrorists don't stay in their lanes." They tend to work together. That includes other groups in Afghanistan besides the Taliban, such as the Haqqani network.[9] The goal of a large, growing fundamentalist movement that would attempt to create a caliphate throughout much of the Islamic world, and use extreme methods against

American allies and interests as well as other dissenting groups and individuals in the process, is not confined to al Qaeda. A victory for the Afghan resistance is effectively a victory, and a major one at that, for al Qaeda and associated movements with a global and anti-Western agenda.

Another crucial reason to prevail in Afghanistan is to prevent Pakistani extremists from using Afghanistan as a sanctuary and training ground for launching attacks against their own country. A destabilized, nuclear-armed Pakistan, with up to 100 nuclear weapons and thousands of extremist fighters including al Qaeda partisans, would be an even greater threat to the United States and other states than would a failed state in Afghanistan itself. Afghanistan is not very far from central Pakistan, and the border regions between the two countries are so hard to police that it would be highly undesirable to allow extremists such a safe haven so close to a strategically crucial state. At precisely the moment when Pakistan is finally committing more of its resources to going after extremists in its own tribal regions, it would be an unfortunate moment to give them a sanctuary within Afghanistan. Moreover, there are growing reasons to fear that Afghan Taliban, Pakistani Taliban, and al Qaeda have developed more links and more forms of cooperation in recent years. This is not a conclusive argument in favor of winning in Afghanistan at all costs, but it is an important reason why defeat would be worrisome.

Some argue that our core goals can be achieved through a more narrow counterterrorism agenda, rather than a full-scale counterinsurgency approach. That is, they favor "CT, not COIN," to use the acronyms commonly employed for each concept. They believe that another 9/11 could be prevented, and major disruption to Pakistan averted, by a more limited approach. Under this strategy, special forces would periodically attack any cells that coalesced within Afghanistan, even in the absence of a stable central government. Drones, cruise missiles, and other forms of standoff attack would contribute as well, carrying out strikes in both Afghanistan and Pakistan. In this way, these critics say, we would accomplish our core objectives without engaging in huge risks to American personnel or unrealistic aspirations about the possibility of helping construct a functioning Afghan state.

But it is the CT plan that is unrealistic. In essence, it is the plan that the Bush administration tried in its early years and that clearly failed, leaving us with the dilemma we have today. To be effective CT must have intelligence, but obtaining solid intelligence on the locations of terrorists is very difficult without a strong presence on the ground and the cooperation of friendly local actors. Such friendly local Afghans are much harder to find, and protect, in a chaotic, destabilized country.[10] At some point, if and when the Afghan resistance prevails in combat, as would likely happen under a CT approach, the air bases and other facilities we currently use to attack extremists in both Afghanistan and Pakistan could also be lost.

Proponents of CT respond that the international community is trying a more minimal approach to countering al Qaeda in places such as Somalia and some of the tribal areas of Yemen—two additional places largely unpoliced by any effective government. If we can get by with such an approach in these places, why not Afghanistan too, one might ask? But Afghanistan is a more remote country than Somalia or Yemen, and a place with more tribal networks and political actors favorable to al Qaeda. As the Bush administration learned, air strikes and commando raids against suspected terror targets are much harder to pull off quickly and effectively in Afghanistan than they would be in other places. Afghanistan is therefore a safer, more convenient place for al Qaeda to operate. And al Qaeda has already proven its interest in operating from Afghanistan. Its leadership remains based nearby in the mountains of western Pakistan even today. There is currently considerable Pakistani action against extremists in these regions, so we finally have a chance to execute a hammer and anvil approach against the major redoubts for al Qaeda and associated movements. To be sure, a CT approach may be our only fallback position if the counterinsurgency effort fails. But it is a poor substitute.

Yet another reason to try to succeed in Afghanistan is to make good on our commitment to an important Muslim people. We owe the Afghans, who have suffered greatly as a pawn in great-power conflict over the last thirty years, a chance at a better future. Their decade-long stand against the Soviet invasion of Afghanistan weakened the Soviet Union and helped us end the cold war. We have a historical debt, therefore, as well as a moral one. It is also worth noting that the Afghans' drug production problem would not exist at today's current scale without a market for illegal narcotics in the Western world, a fact that further implicates us in Afghanistan's fate and deepens our moral responsibility. For one of us, this is an especially personal argument, but the point has importance regardless, given America's values and its role in the world as a beacon of democracy and human rights. Americans cannot build a new Afghanistan themselves, of course; only Afghans can do that. But the United States, as well as the broader international community, has a certain moral obligation to give them a chance to do so. This is not an argument for staying forever, but it is an argument for trying to do the job right before going home. In addition to its moral attributes, such a strategy can help counter (at least somewhat) those cynics who falsely claim that the United States does not care about the well-being of Muslim peoples and only uses them for its own Machiavellian purposes. Such arguments, reinforced by the stalemate in the Israeli-Palestinian peace process, hurt the United States because they help al Qaeda and related groups recruit followers.[11]

There is admittedly a flip side to this argument, however: if the Afghan people and, more to the point, the Afghan government fail to do their part in this war, the American moral commitment at some point will no longer be so binding. To put it differently, the United States and other countries could try their utmost and still fail because of mistakes made by President Hamid Karzai and other Afghan officials—and at that point, there would be little point in further investments in failure. Other means of stabilizing Pakistan, the most crucial country in the region for American strategic interests, would have to be explored. It is important that President Karzai understand this, rather than view the international commitment to his country as open-ended, because his administration has a crucial role to play in improving our strategy in Afghanistan. But it would clearly be much better to succeed in Afghanistan, thereby depriving al Qaeda of a new sanctuary and a major propaganda victory and preventing Pakistani Taliban from gaining another redoubt of their own.

WHY WE CAN SUCCEED

The Afghan people, working with the international community, have a very good chance to succeed in this war. Success means defeating or at least containing the insurgency, gradually improving law and order, and creating infrastructure to allow for economic progress. The road will not be easy, and the outcome will not be a prosperous Western-style democracy. Secretary Gates was surely right when he said that there will be no "Valhalla" in Central Asia. But we can help the Afghans build a viable state that over time can increasingly control its territory and improve the lives of its people.

This may seem a modest set of goals. But if we can attain them, it would prevent Afghanistan from becoming a place where 9/11-type attacks are again planned and organized. It also would literally keep alive future generations of Afghan peoples—in contrast to the last thirty years. Since the Soviets invaded in 1979, well over 1 million have died from violence, while nearly all the rest have lived in extreme poverty and deprivation.

Here are some reasons to hope for success. First, Afghans want a better future for themselves. This is true for Afghans who remain in their own country, as well as for the diaspora of Afghans around the world—many of whom have moved back home to help build a new country, others of whom stand ready to invest and trade and assist in other ways. Most Afghans reject war. They also reject the Taliban, by 90 percent or more in most polls. Among the majority of the Afghan people who are not Pashtun, in fact, support for the Taliban is virtually zero.[12] Even among the Durrani, one of the two main Pashtun tribal groupings, support for the Taliban has been limited (the Taliban's main support has come from the Pashtun Ghilzai tribes).[13] In Kandahar City, the base for Taliban operations before they were ousted in 2001 and a central focus of the current insurgency, Taliban support reached an all-time high of 25 percent in 2009—but even there, three of every four Afghans had a favorable opinion of the government.[14] The Ulema Council of Afghanistan and other important religious groups also have supported the Afghan government and criticized the Taliban.[15]

In fact, the Taliban is not a popular insurgency. It is in equal parts a narcoterrorist organization willing to use drug smuggling to finance its operations, an extremist Islamist movement with an intolerant view of nonbelievers and a backward view of the role of women in society, and a ruthless organization willing to use brutal violence against innocent, law-abiding citizens to impose its version of Islam.

There is no clear consensus for Afghans on where to go from here. They are angry with the international community, and to a lesser extent with President Karzai, for doing a poor job in helping them build a viable state over the last eight years. And among some Afghans, that anger sometimes translates into support for insurgents—at least locally and temporarily. But it does not mean the Afghan people want a return to the communist rule of the late 1970s and 1980s, or the anarchy and bloodletting of the late 1980s and early 1990s, or the tyranny of the Taliban thereafter.

Despite being devastated by thirty years of war, Afghans are resolute, resourceful, and proud people. They have a real sense of national history and identity, even if some aspects of their nationalism have been weakened by decades of conflict and need to be rebuilt. They are a young, forward-looking people—70 percent of the population is under thirty and nearly one-third of all citizens now live in cities. They are indeed good fighters, but they are not the caricature of backward, xenophobic warriors so often portrayed in the mass media.[16] They are aware of the opportunity promised by a modern, democratic government supported by a strong economy and an educated population. There are many good people in positions of power in government, as well as in the private sector and civil society. The promising performance of the Afghan National Army also suggests that it is in fact possible to build viable, national institutions—that the country is more than a collection of tribes with no regard for central authority and no sense of Afghan identity.

There are also many good and committed "average citizens." In Kandahar City citizens are telling authorities about the locations of up to 80 percent of all improvised explosive devices before they go off, allowing security forces to defuse them. This high percentage, higher than ever witnessed in Iraq, further suggests that our efforts to quell the Taliban may have found unexpected support from the general population in one of the Taliban strongholds, support that a counterinsurgency can build upon. Progress is apparent in other places too. In the town of Nawa in Helmand Province, for example, an infusion of U.S. forces in 2009 has turned a previously lawless area held by the Taliban into a relatively secure area where ordinary people can begin to get back to their daily lives.[17]

Second, elements of the Afghan security forces are improving fast. This is most true for the army, and for some police units that have received intensive oversight and mentoring through programs like the Focused District Development effort. With NATO's International Security Assistance Force (ISAF) focused intently now on proper training and mentoring, the building of Afghan security forces that can protect their own people should accelerate.

Third, life in Afghanistan has actually improved somewhat compared with the recent past. As bad as many security trends have been, for most Afghans the country is far less violent today than it was in the 1980s and 1990s. Actual violence levels are probably worse than official statistics report, as acknowledged by ISAF documents, but they are still roughly comparable to those in Iraq today—meaning violence in Afghanistan today is ten times less than it was in Iraq before the surge.[18] Of course the situation in Afghanistan is different, and in some ways the Taliban is a smarter foe than was al Qaeda in Iraq—generally avoiding the truck bombings that kill dozens and embitter the population, while spreading its influence more insidiously. Still, it is important to realize that the country is not being ripped apart before our eyes, as Iraq was in the 2004–06 period.

Life in Afghanistan today is better in material terms too. Yes, the progress is uneven, and the poor remain very badly off. But overall the economy, education, health care, and similar indicators are moving more in the right direction than the wrong one. Material progress has contributed to a reservoir of good will among the Afghan people toward those in authority. President Karzai, the United States, and NATO all still enjoyed at least 60 percent support from the population as of summer 2009—far better than the United States has enjoyed in Iraq.[19] This popularity number is fragile, and uneven among different groups, but we do have some advantages in how the Afghan public views the situation nonetheless.

Fourth, NATO in general and the United States in particular know how to carry out counterinsurgency missions better than ever before. Many troops are now knowledgeable about Afghanistan too. We also have excellent commanders, starting with Central Command Combatant Commander General David Petraeus and General McChrystal, who directs both the NATO forces and the separate, U.S.-led counterterrorism force carrying out Operation Enduring Freedom there.[20] Commanders at much lower levels of authority—the ones who execute the strategy day in and day out—are also seasoned. The importance of good leadership in counterinsurgency is very significant, and our strengths in this area are a major asset.[21] Recent progress is increasingly apparent in some places such as Helmand, Wardak, and Logar provinces as a result.

Fifth, much of the basic strategy announced in March 2009 and reaffirmed by President Obama on Decmeber 1 is finally right. After seven years of treating Afghanistan as the forgotten war, the United States is seriously resourcing its effort there with combat troops, trainers for Afghan forces, development aid, top-notch leadership, and other capabilities. In mid-2008 the chairman of the Joint Chiefs of Staff, Admiral Michael Mullen, said, "Afghanistan has been and remains an economy-of-force campaign, which by definition means we need more forces there."[22] He was even more blunt in December 2007, when he said, "In

Afghanistan, we do what we can. In Iraq, we do what we must."[23] On the ground, this reality prevented combined Afghan and NATO forces from securing many districts, towns, and villages. It left troops stalemated in dangerous situations over extended periods of time because they did not have the capacity to seize land and sustain control. It left NATO forces relying too heavily on air strikes with all their potential to cause accidental deaths of innocents (a policy that McChrystal has changed; dangerous air strikes are generally allowed now only if NATO troops are in direct peril).[24] And it left Afghan citizens who cooperate with NATO and their government vulnerable to reprisal.[25] Only in 2009 did these realities finally begin to change.

Historically, only 40 percent of modern counterinsurgencies have succeeded (and somewhat less in the most recent times), according to work by Jason Lyall, Isaiah Wilson, and Ivan Arreguin-Toft. However, 70 percent of the counterinsurgencies that focused on population security have been effective, according to research by Andrew Enterline and Joseph Magagnoli. Given the degree of commitment and excellence of U.S. and other NATO forces today, the odds would seem at least that great in our favor today—provided everyone, including the Afghan government, can work together in support of the basic strategy.[26]

WHY WE COULD FAIL

For all the promise, Afghanistan could still fail—meaning a return to civil war, or a takeover by extremists and tyrants, some of whom would be allied with al Qaeda. Any such outcome would provide the potential for al Qaeda to reestablish a sanctuary in Afghanistan, meaning that the United States and its allies would fail as well, and their security would be put at greater risk.

Despite its limitations, the Taliban-led insurgency has many strengths. It is well organized, cunningly led, and increasingly confident. Its use of roadside bombs and small-unit ambushes imperils NATO and Afghan troops. It has ample access to weapons and explosives, given the huge stocks of weaponry still scattered throughout the country from previous conflicts, and the numerous smuggling routes across Central Asia.[27] Afghans sense that the insurgency has momentum and are drawn to it for that reason. The Taliban have a shadow government structure, run out of Quetta, Pakistan, by what is famously known as the Quetta *shura*, or leadership group, which maintains a system of governance throughout key parts of Pashtun-run Afghanistan (primarily the south and east of the country). While the Taliban may be corrupt in their reliance on drug money, they are by most accounts not corrupt in their interactions with normal Afghan citizens, who often comment that the Taliban operate with more discipline, and demand fewer bribes, than do government officials or police forces. The Taliban now operate in more than one-third of Afghanistan's nearly 400 districts. Their chilling use of "night letters," assassinations, and other forms of intimidation sows terror among local leaders as well as the general population, allowing the Taliban to maneuver relatively freely. By avoiding the mass atrocities used against civilian populations by other insurgencies, the Taliban may also have mitigated some of the anger that would otherwise have been directed against them.

This leads directly to the second and related problem: the Taliban's ability to gain supporters among the growing number of Afghans disgusted by the government's incompetence and corruption (and by policy mistakes by the international community). If the government continues to flounder, there could come a day when, for many Afghans, the Taliban seem the lesser of two evils.[28] Indeed, that is already the case for tribes that feel disenfranchised by the Karzai government. Tribes that feel badly served by the current government, and upset by the benefits that rival tribes may enjoy through patronage, are already inclined to support the resistance.[29]

Corruption permeates many Afghan institutions, not least of which is the police force. In the eyes of most Afghans, the police force is a corrupt and distrusted organization. According to one 2009 survey, by Carol Graham and Soumya Chattopadhyay, while 69 percent of Afghans said they trusted the army, only 21 percent trusted the police.[30] That Afghanistan produces 90 percent of the world's opium, and that its farmers have relatively few alternatives to growing poppy reinforces the problem of corruption and lawlessness—many police are drug users themselves and are susceptible to bribes. The drug trade is well organized in Afghanistan now, with twenty-five to thirty key trafficking networks operational, most based in Kandahar.[31] This culture is part of a broader problem of lawlessness; even if the Afghanistan war per se is not as violent as many other conflicts, the frequency of kidnappings, robberies, and other crimes enormously weakens public morale and support for the government.[32] The police must be reformed even as its size is perhaps nearly doubled in the coming years, out of a population with relatively few potential recruits who are literate.

The crime problem is exacerbated by the ever-present risk that key Afghan leaders, in government and out, will be assassinated or driven from the country by fear. In addition to making reform difficult, the loss of leaders is especially worrisome given the country's shortage of experienced leaders and managers after thirty years of war. In the government, in particular, there is often a good minister at the top of a given organization but weak second- and third-tier leadership.[33] The problem is compounded when the country's middle and upper classes give up hope and leave for destinations abroad. This trend has been accelerating in recent years; for example, 18,000 Afghans applied for asylum in Europe in 2008, nearly twice the number as in 2007.[34]

A third central concern is that the international effort is not yet solid. That is true despite the reforms introduced by General McChrystal on the military side of the operation. International aid and development activities remain poorly coordinated. U.S. and NATO troops often clear areas of enemy forces but then must wait long periods before international or Afghan civilian efforts begin in earnest. In addition, international aid organizations often contribute, indirectly and unintentionally, to the culture of corruption by providing contracts to cronies of the current political leadership and thereby indirectly disadvantaging other Afghans, who become angry with prevailing power structures and more supportive of the insurgency as a result. This pattern is common with contracts for construction and related services.

Also troublesome are the CIA's reported payments to President Karzai's brother, Ahmed Wali Karzai, who is widely believed to be involved in drug dealing in southern Afghanistan. Wali Karzai reportedly has helped the CIA work with a local militia group in the area. But the costs outweigh the benefits. The overall effort in the south of Afghanistan has been failing largely because association with such individuals discredits the Afghan government and the international community and thus generates support for the insurgency. In defending such practices, and perhaps attempting to sound realistic and savvy about the ways of the country, one unnamed intelligence source was reported to have said that "if you're looking for Mother Teresa, she doesn't live in Afghanistan." But that comment is naïve in its suggestion that there are no huge consequences to working with such corrupt individuals. Closer to the mark was the comment of Major General Michael Flynn, the top intelligence officer for ISAF, who stated that "the only way to clean up Chicago is to get rid of Capone." The international community has not yet acted on such advice itself—which puts it in a weak position to demand greater anticorruption efforts from President Karzai.[35]

Pakistan poses a fourth major challenge. It has about 25 million Pashtuns, roughly double the number in Afghanistan—a significant number given that the Taliban in particular are a Pashtun-based movement.[36] Pakistan represents a sanctuary for elements of the Afghan insurgency (clustered largely in Quetta, near the border with Afghanistan's Kandahar Province and where the Afghan Taliban is headquartered, and in Peshawar near the Pakistani end of the Khyber Pass, where other militias have their headquarters as well). Particularly in the south of Afghanistan, most resistance fighters are indigenous Afghans. But some fighters do cross the border from Pakistan into Afghanistan to fight, especially in the east of the country. So do weapons. Pakistan's Inter-Services Intelligence Directorate, or ISI, is believed to still support some actions taken by the Taliban and other militias—as for example in the July 7, 2008, suicide bombing of the Indian embassy in Kabul, which killed more than 50.[37] In addition, Pakistan's Frontier Corps is believed to have provided supporting fire from border posts for certain insurgent operations within Afghanistan.[38]

These four major risks on the ground produce in turn a fifth major threat to the mission: a collapse of support for the effort in the Western world and particularly in the United States. We are writing this book largely in the hope of helping to boost support for the counterinsurgency. But if battlefield trends continue as they did into 2009, it will be increasingly hard to sustain support for the effort in the West. The growing sense that the Afghan leadership is working with brutal warlords and corrupt drug dealers, and was willing even to consider stealing a presidential election to remain in power, further undercuts support for the mission. It also casts fundamental doubt on the viability of the mission, because no counterinsurgency effort can succeed without a credible indigenous partner to outside forces. The Karzai government has not been performing up to par. If it continues on its current path, the effort to build a functioning Afghan state that can contain the insurgency increasingly on its own is highly unlikely to succeed. That said, we should also recall that President Karzai has appointed some reformers and good leaders, even if more must be done.

These are all serious problems. But there is encouraging news too. For example, U.S. political support for the mission is likely to continue at some level for a time, even if it is begrudging and gradually weakening.

Major Roads in Afghanistan

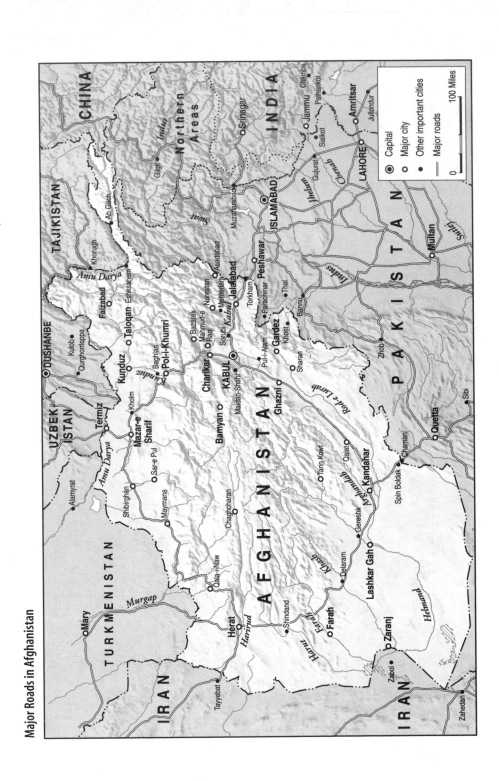

That is because the 9/11 attacks originated from Afghanistan and because President Obama has made the Afghanistan-Pakistan theater the core of his national security strategy. Reform of the Afghan police will be hard. But the Afghan army is showing considerable competence, and even the police are improving when they receive adequate training, mentoring, and partnering. Anticorruption campaigns that target and fire the worst offenders, create stronger offices of inspector general in key parts of government, mount vigorous public information campaigns, and most of all hire credible people for key leadership positions have worked reasonably well from Singapore to Botswana to Uganda to parts of Iraq's government, so we have some models to follow.[39] New economic opportunities can be created with projected improvements in irrigation and transportation systems—systems that NATO and Afghan forces should now have the manpower to protect more effectively. Assassinations and kidnappings are always a worry, and a serious one, but again, the capacity to protect is growing. Pakistan is a real threat in providing (or at least failing to deny) sanctuary for Afghan resistance leaders and allowing weapons as well as Taliban fighters to cross the border. But the government now seems more serious about the threats to its own internal security than before.

Ultimately, perhaps the best way to sum up the situation is to say that the Afghanistan mission is a race against time. Stalemate works to the advantage of the enemy. Not only does it weaken public support in the United States and elsewhere in the Western world, it engenders bitterness on the part of the Afghan people toward NATO forces and their own government. Indeed, in recent years the situation has not been stalemating; it has been worsening. Despite economic progress, the security situation has clearly deteriorated. The addition of 30,000 more American troops in 2009 has led to a certain degree of localized stabilization in parts of the country, but overall trends remain mediocre if somewhat better than before. High-profile issues such as air strikes that cause civilian fatalities have also had huge and disproportionate resonance throughout Afghanistan and sparked anger against those carrying them out; as Admiral Mullen said after one such tragic incident in May of 2009, "We can't keep going through incidents like this and expect the strategy to work."[40] Improvements are already happening on the ground. But success is not preordained, and we could still lose.

Ethnolinguistic Groups in Afghanistan

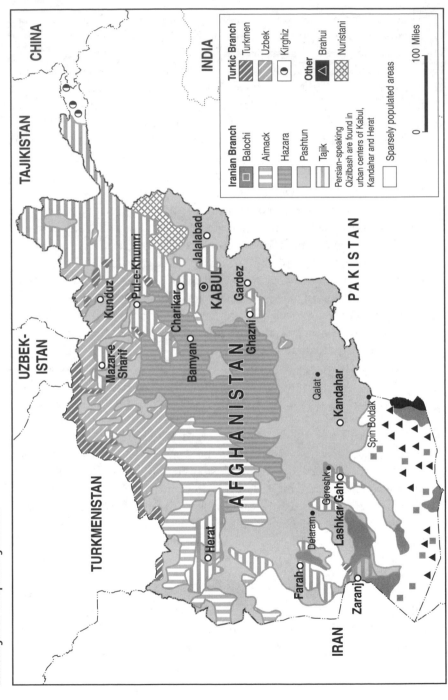

CHAPTER TWO

The Rise, Fall, and Resurgence of the Taliban

How did Afghanistan end up in its current troubled state? And how have the Taliban become such a powerful, resurgent force within the country—with continuing strong links to al Qaeda as well as to the Pakistani Taliban and elements of the Pakistan intelligence community? If we are to assess accurately the prospects for success, we must first understand the foe we face.

The Taliban are an impressive and resilient movement and a formidable adversary of the Afghan people, the United States, NATO, and the broader international community. Their goal is to impose, once again, an extremist view of Islam on Afghanistan, where the country is run by religious leaders and citizens are forced, through often harsh and even brutal intimidation, to adhere to religious tenets and rules of life, and where dissent is not tolerated. Only by understanding the way the Taliban gain support through a combination of intimidation, indoctrination, discipline, and battlefield momentum can we learn how to challenge them. And only by understanding what the country of Afghanistan has suffered in the last thirty years can we appreciate the degree of the challenge involved in trying to rebuild it.

Some say that Afghanistan has never been a functioning state. That is not really correct. It is true that, in the distant past, the lands making up Afghanistan were a crossroads of invaders and civilizations. Genghis Khan and Tamerlane were among the invaders, and Arabs, Mongols, Persians, and Uzbeks were all influential at one time or another. Islam began to spread into Afghanistan shortly after the Prophet Muhammad died in 632 and over time began to provide a certain glue for the country. Kabul and other parts of central and southern Afghanistan remained largely Buddhist until the twelfth century, when they were either conquered by Islamic rulers or converted.[1]

By the eighteenth century, a weak central government, controlled by the Pashtun, ruled the country. The Pashtun ethnic group is divided into several tribal groups, dominated in Afghanistan by two main tribal confederations that have often struggled with each other for control: the Durrani (President Hamid Karzai is Durrani) and the Ghilzai (most recruits to the Taliban are Ghilzai). Not all small tribes belong to one confederation or the other, however.

In the nineteenth century, Afghanistan became a focal point of the "great game" between Britain and Russia for influence in the region.[2] Ultimately, the British won and imposed the so-called Durand Line in 1893, dividing the Pashtun people between two different countries in the process—Afghanistan and that portion of India that became Pakistan in 1947.[3] Afghanistan gained its independence from Britain in 1919, and was ruled as a monarchy until the early 1970s.

The modern history—and turbulent era—of Afghan politics began later in the 1970s, when a flirtation by one Afghan leader with socialist ideas precipitated a period of coups, assassinations, and, in 1979, an invasion by the Soviet Union. Since then, Afghanistan has been in a state of nearly continuous war, and close to two million have died from violence.[4] Much of the fighting and dying occurred against the Soviets. Resistance fighters, commonly known as mujahedin, with American, Saudi, and Pakistani assistance, fought and bled the Soviets until Mikhail Gorbachev finally pulled out the Soviet troops in February 1989. As one indication of the scale of effort, and the perceived stakes in this cold war battle, the United States and Saudi Arabia are estimated to have each given $4 billion or more in aggregate aid over that period.[5] The war was brutal, especially for the Afghan people. In addition to war fatalities, another seven million to eight million Afghans—roughly half the population—were driven from their homes; five million of these fled abroad as refugees. (Afghans now number about 30 million.)

The tragedy continued after the Soviet pullout. For several years, Najibullah, Afghanistan's Soviet-backed leader since 1986, fought to remain in power against an assortment of warlords and mujahedin (although the distinction between the two categories is often blurry).[6]

After he was overthrown in 1992, the victorious mujahedin leaders agreed to share power with each other through a rotating presidency, but this approach did not work. Some former mujahedin as well as a motley crew of others turned to warlordism. Individuals including Abdul Rashid Dostum, Ismail Khan, and Gulbuddin Hekmatyar turned the country into a Hobbesian world of anarchy and brutality.[7] Outside powers contributed to the mayhem that ensued after the Soviet withdrawal, backing various sides. Notably, India and Pakistan were both inclined to support whoever the other side did not favor.[8] The United States hardly deserved any praise itself; with the Soviets gone, Washington's interest in the country was minimal, driven by residual anticommunist sentiment; it was blind to the consequences of the ongoing civil strife for the well-being of the Afghan people. As a result, anarchy prevailed, and the country remained in a state of severe underdevelopment.[9]

The anticommunist agenda of the United States in Afghanistan led Washington to provide just enough support to militia leaders to help them weaken and later overthrow the Najibullah government—but not enough resources or diplomatic engagement to help build something positive in the communist regime's place. In the end, this realpolitik was not as savvy or hard-headed as the term implies. It helped foster the conditions that later contributed to 9/11. And it foreshadowed in some ways what would happen after 9/11 and the overthrow of the Taliban.

Anarchy reigned until the Taliban—the word literally means *students*—emerged in 1994. The Taliban included some of the mujahedin who fought against the Soviets, as well as a wide range of others. The Taliban spread through much of the country over the next year and by 1998 also ruled key northern cities. By the turn of the decade, only the Panshjir Valley northeast of Kabul and nearby areas were outside Taliban control. It was in Panshjir that the Northern Alliance, under Ahmed Shah Massoud and composed largely of Tajiks, Uzbeks, and Hazaras, maintained its base of operations. Massoud was assassinated by al Qaeda operatives two days before 9/11, but the Northern Alliance nonetheless later teamed with American forces to overthrow the Taliban in late 2001.

Many Afghans initially welcomed the Taliban in the mid-1990s, because of their strong emphasis on law and order, but the harshness of the Taliban rule soon turned these feelings into disgust and fear. The United States occasionally contemplated reaching out to the Taliban, out of hope that the movement might moderate. More importantly, however, Pakistan gave support to the movement. For Pakistan, the Taliban provided a potential pool of extremists willing to attack India in Kashmir and elsewhere in the name of Islam, while also preventing a pro-India government from becoming established in Kabul. In fact, elements of the Pakistani state such as the Inter-Services Intelligence Directorate are believed to still offer support to the movement. Islamabad's support for the Taliban created elements of distrust between Pakistan and subsequent Afghan governments that are only now beginning to soften.[10]

From the mid-1990s onward, the Taliban allied with the al Qaeda terrorists who attacked, among other targets, the U.S. embassies in Kenya and Tanzania in 1998 as well as targets in New York and Washington on September 11, 2001. These bonds between the Taliban and al Qaeda have only strengthened since.

In addition to the obvious devastation from so many years of war, this legacy of conflict has wrecked Afghanistan's legitimate economy. Most of what drives the economy now is opium revenue, international aid, and the trickle-down stimulus effects of the large international military and civilian presence in the country. To some extent, this is unsurprising for an inland nation that is extremely mountainous and quite dry, with only 10 to 15 percent of all land arable for farming. But Afghanistan has in the past been a land of pomegranate and other orchards, grains, and other agricultural production. In fact, its climate is reasonably good for growing crops—sunny and fairly warm in the summer in much of the country. Extensive irrigation made it quite productive in the past, and it could be again, although that would require repairing the dams and canals, making the roads safe, and replanting the orchards. These things in turn require stanching the insurgency, or at least checking its growing momentum. Why hasn't this happened yet?

AFGHANISTAN IN BUSH'S FIRST TERM: THE "LIGHT FOOTPRINT"

A small American-dominated foreign military mission, including intelligence operatives, worked with the Northern Alliance and other resistance groups to overthrow the Taliban in October and November of 2001. Before that point, Taliban forces probably numbered around 30,000. But as they lost the key battles, many Taliban fighters "went to ground" and stopped supporting the movement; many of its top leaders along with al Qaeda fled to Pakistan's nearby mountainous tribal regions.

Once the Taliban was deposed and it became apparent that Osama bin Laden was in hiding in Pakistan, the U.S. military effort became quite limited—the strategy espoused a "light footprint" and a minimalist approach. International economic and development aid was also modest in scope. The desire for a small military footprint was motivated in part by the Bush administration's aversion to nation building, in part by Secretary of Defense Donald Rumsfeld's desire to validate a new kind of warfare that deemphasized ground forces, and in part by incipient planning for the Iraq invasion. The broader lack of interest in Afghanistan's welfare was consistent with America's long-standing view of Afghanistan as a country of limited strategic importance. The United States was more interested in opposing and tearing down things it did not like there—starting with the Soviet occupation itself, then the Soviet-installed communist government, and then the Taliban—than in building up anything viable to replace these enemy regimes.

At the Bonn Conference of December 2001, which involved many nations including Iran as well as representatives of many Afghan groups, Hamid Karzai was selected to be Afghanistan's interim leader, a choice that most Afghans and many countries favored. Karzai attempted to appoint a cabinet reflective of the ethnic balance of Afghanistan. This objective may have been well intentioned, but it also had the negative effect of creating a quota system that sometimes precluded putting the best people into key jobs.[11] His government was also understaffed and under-resourced. Much of Washington's interest in this phase of the effort was in working with regional warlords to continue to pursue al Qaeda operatives, an approach that tended to further undercut the central government.

Various positive steps were taken. In 2004 a new constitution written by the Afghan Constitution Commission was approved by a traditional Afghan mechanism known as a *loya jirga*.[12] Later that year, Karzai was elected president in a national election. Parliamentary elections were held in September 2005. Outside countries gradually increased their commitments and aid to Afghanistan as well. However, they tended to do so at a pace slower than the situation required—and not fast enough to keep the Taliban from regrouping.

From 2002 through 2005, U.S. troop levels grew from around 5,000 to 19,000, as the security situation worsened somewhat and efforts to build up Afghan security forces and extend the reach of the central government gradually increased.[13] In August 2003 NATO officially took command of the International Security Assistance Force that had been established under a U.N. mandate in Kabul in 2002. ISAF included some American troops, but others remained organized (and commanded) separately in a counterterrorism operation that continued to be known as Operation Enduring Freedom. In 2004 ISAF began gradually to assume responsibility for security outside of the capital, first setting up a base in the relatively peaceful north. By October 2006 ISAF had taken over security responsibility throughout Afghanistan, breaking the country up into five regional commands (East, West, North, South, and Central). But these trends did not change the fact that, for a country of 30 million people, the NATO-ISAF capabilities were still meager. And while monthly fatalities for foreign troops rarely exceeded single digits, casualty trends were inching upward.[14]

U.S.-NATO efforts to build Afghan security forces were modest as well. By the end of 2005 only 50,000 Afghan forces (comprising both the army and national police) were assigned to duty throughout the country; even fewer were competent, equipped, and reliable. In these early years of the war, the so-called lead nation concept was employed, under which different countries took responsibility for different main tasks within the country—the United States oversaw the creation and training of the Afghan army; Germany, the police; Japan, the disarmament of militias; the United Kingdom, counternarcotics efforts; and Italy, the justice system. This effort was poorly coordinated and later judged largely unsuccessful.[15]

AFGHANISTAN SINCE 2005: AMERICA GRADUALLY GETS SERIOUS—BUT SO DOES THE ENEMY

Over time, even as foreign troop capabilities grew, the security situation in Afghanistan continued to worsen. During the second half of the decade, a clear trend has emerged—the economy and quality of life, as measured in material terms in general, are gradually improving while security is deteriorating. Since 2007 the worsening security situation has begun to predominate, threatening continued improvement in the economy.

Consider the situation in early 2010. From a security standpoint, by almost any measurement 2008 and 2009 represent the most violent years since the onset of the war in 2001. For example, in 2008 American and coalition troops suffered 294 deaths, a 27 percent increase over 2007. And in 2009, coalition losses were about 500, with U.S. fatalities exceeding 300. These numbers remain significantly smaller than the annual average of 800 deaths that U.S. troops in Iraq suffered until 2008, but relative to the overall size of deployed forces, losses in Afghanistan have become comparable to those the United States suffered in Iraq during that war's first few years. Afghan security forces have been losing about 1,000 personnel a year, most in the police force.

For the Afghan civilian population, the situation also is worsening. Violence levels are still not horribly high in an absolute sense—compared, for example, with those in Iraq before the surge, or with Afghanistan's own violence levels during the past three decades. But security forces and government officials are in dire danger, kidnappings are up, and in many places citizens can use roads only by paying bribes, often to the police. In contrast to Iraq's recent past, Afghanistan does not have many of the big car bombings or deliberate stokings of sectarian strife by groups seeking to spark a cycle of revenge and counterrevenge. Yet it does have the kinds of targeted insurgent activity that prevent the government from establishing control of the country, limit the potential for economic growth, and discourage reformers.

The Taliban have not engaged in the widespread terrorist acts that plagued Iraq. Instead, their use of threats in the form of anonymous "night letters" delivered to the homes of those loyal to the government, together with occasional assassinations of those disregarding the threats, has killed or driven away many good Afghans who wanted to help reform and rebuild their country and has intimidated those who remain. Indeed, the Afghan Taliban's care in using force may make it more formidable than any one (or all) of the various insurgencies within Iraq, because it limits the population's anger at the movement.

Afghanistan's multiple insurgent groups do not generally coordinate operations or recognize a common leader. The Taliban-led insurgency in the south, coordinated out of Quetta, Pakistan, by the so-called Quetta shura, is an exception. For several years now, under the general leadership of Mullah Omar (who may now be in Karachi, Pakistan) and day-to-day operational management of Mullah Barader, this group has developed annual strategy plans; maintained shadow governments in most of Afghanistan and tracked their performance; and revised its strategy as needed.[16] It provides an alternative judicial system for many of the people of southern Afghanistan, especially in rural areas, and does so in a way generally seen as somewhat fair—if harsh and blunt. It has taken some of the edge off its brutal methods and extreme rhetoric of past years—at least for now—and sought to avoid antagonizing non-Pashtun groups as well.[17] Even though illegal narcotics contribute to its coffers, its officials and partisans are motivated more by ideology, and less by greed, than many in the government. As a result, many normal citizens have come to prefer Taliban justice to the system of bribes, nepotism, and other favoritism that predominates in many places where the government is in charge.[18]

Taliban fighters also have improved their battlefield tactics. Several years ago they would sometimes mass for battle, perhaps sensing a growing momentum nationwide. But they would generally lose the ensuing firefights—if not right away, then once NATO reinforcements arrived to back up Afghan forces or smaller foreign units initially engaged by the insurgents. For example, in 2006 the Taliban sought to establish control in a large swath of the south of the country but were defeated by a combination of Canadian, other NATO, and Afghan forces.[19] Since then, coordinated actions of large numbers of Taliban fighters have sometimes occurred—but generally in places where insurgent forces realized they could challenge a small NATO outpost, as with the summer 2008 battles in eastern Afghanistan (such as the "Battle of Wanat") and a similar mass attack, also in the east, on October 4, 2009.[20] Most other operations have been conducted by small numbers of individuals. Often their approach is a complex ambush, using the detonation of a roadside bomb to create initial injury and panic, and then quickly moving in with small-arms fire against the incapacitated vehicle or vehicles and their NATO or Afghan soldiers or police.

As of late 2009, NATO intelligence estimated that the insurgency might include roughly 25,000 dedicated, full-time fighters, nearly the Taliban's pre-9/11 level. The Taliban and other resistance groups are also seen by many Afghans as having the battlefield momentum. As a result, many individuals—and tribes—split their loyalties to hedge their bets. A leader from the Popalzai tribe of Pashtun in Uruzgan Province, north of Kandahar where the Dutch and Australians operate, put it this way: "As a tribe, we cannot afford to be seen as favoring one side rather than the other. Of course, we have Popalzai within the insurgency ranks, as much as we have many of our tribesmen working for the government; no one knows what will happen in the future."[21]

As for the Taliban's goals, control of Kandahar is probably their first and main interest, given the area's historical, religious, economic, and cultural importance to the Taliban.[22] The Taliban appear to be trying to approach Kandahar from various directions out of their sanctuary in Pakistan—having done so first through Uruzgan Province to the north of Kandahar and more recently through Helmand Province to the west. As they ensconce themselves and increase their strength, they are then in an increasingly good position to employ assassinations and other intimidation methods to try to pry the population away from loyalty to the government—even as NATO watches from close by.

Despite increases in U.S. and NATO forces, numbering more than 100,000 as of early 2010, with a total of 140,000 troops expected by summer, Afghan citizens increasingly blame the Western forces as well as their own corrupt and dysfunctional government for the deterioration in the security environment. NATO air strikes are often seen as contributing callously (if accidentally) to civilian casualties. Several specific incidents in which large numbers of civilians have been killed by NATO bombs have roused ire among Afghans. Most of these air strikes have been called in to protect NATO and Afghan troops under fire, but they sometimes have been based on bad intelligence—or perhaps even deliberate disinformation from insurgents trying to provoke NATO to kill innocents inadvertently, or from one tribe trying to settle scores with another.[23] The use of airpower is changing under General McChrystal, but it will be hard to change Afghans' perceptions of NATO's disregard for their well-being and their safety.

Just as troubling as trends in the actual security environment are the difficulties of helping Afghans build up their own security forces. There has been some progress, especially with the Afghan army. But substantial problems remain. Recruiting has gone badly in key southern regions like Kandahar and Helmand, suggesting an inability to create patriotic support for the army among some elements of Pashtun populations. Desertion rates have been high, and units sent to combat-intensive areas have been overdeployed and overused, with high casualty rates and insufficient numbers of personnel to compensate for losses. NATO trainers, organized into Operational Mentor and Liaison Teams (or OMLTs, pronounced *omelettes*), not only have been inadequate in number but have not synchronized their schedules with those of the Afghan units they mentor. As a result military advisory teams have often rotated out at critical moments. Training regimens have been reasonable in theory (for both army and police): basic warrior training of ten weeks for all recruits, in Kabul or at a regional facility such as Gardez, Mazar-i-Sharif, or Herat, followed by six to eight weeks of additional specialized training for about 30 percent of the force. But the ability to train enough troops—and most of all, to mentor them in the field thereafter—has been wanting.[24]

The Afghan police, including regular officers as well as the border police, pose even larger problems. Illiteracy, drug abuse, and corruption are rampant in the ranks.[25] Plagued by years of mismanagement and a dearth of resources, the efforts to grow the Afghan National Police (ANP) have thus far yielded a force of modest size that is largely unable to carry out its mandate. The force currently numbers nearly 100,000, making it roughly as large as the Afghan army. But the latest data show that approximately 85 percent are officially judged to be incapable of basic police work, and only about 20 to 25 percent have typically received any training at all. One contributing factor has been a significant shortage of available trainers (again, as with the army, some trainers carry out basic instruction, while others form into small teams called Police Operational Mentor and Liaison Teams, or "pomelettes"). The initial program was, as noted, entrusted to Germany. But it was so underresourced that one German general classified it "a miserable failure."[26] The European Union's European Police, or EUPOL, took a lead role in training the ANP in June 2007, but it too has been unable to provide adequate manpower. Although the mission boasts twenty-one contributing nations, the total number of trainers in Afghanistan at any one time has rarely exceeded 120, well below the stated objective of 400. In November 2008 Major General Robert Cone, then the U.S. commander of the Combined Security Transition Command-Afghanistan, stated that 2,300 more international trainers were needed to train the ANP.[27] Embedded trainers have been particularly scarce. Since President Obama announced a new strategy in March 2009, those realities have begun to change, but they still remain painfully real.

From an economic standpoint, the picture is not as bad. Some indicators such as overall economic growth, per capita income, and volume of trade have risen steadily over the last few years while inflation has largely stabilized. Afghanistan remains very poor. But according to government statistics, more than 80 percent of the Afghan population now lives in districts that have a basic package of health-care programs, up considerably from 9 percent in 2003. This has translated into significant improvements in the rate of vaccinations as well as a decline in infant and child mortality rates. Nearly 7 million children currently attend over 9,000 schools, compared with fewer than 1 million during the Taliban period. Gender equity is improving; more than 2 million of the students are girls, and 40,000 of the 142,000 teachers are women. Telephone usage has increased dramatically, to an estimated 7 million Afghans, compared with 1 million in 2002.

The international community deserves a good deal of credit for what progress has occurred, even if it has not done nearly enough. Aid efforts gradually expanded after the United Nations Assistance Mission in Afghanistan was created in March 2002. After presidential and parliamentary elections in 2004 and 2005, the international community pledged about $10 billion as part of an Afghanistan Compact with the Karzai government.[28] Also in 2002, the provincial reconstruction team (PRT) concept was developed. A PRT is a team of experts charged with kick-starting development efforts even under difficult security conditions and with helping to strengthen local governments by providing advice and prompt resources as well. Eight PRTs were operating by late 2003 and fourteen by late 2004, in large part thanks to Lieutenant General David Barno, who promoted the concept assertively when he was commander of the ISAF mission.[29] At this point in early 2010, twenty-six PRTs are operating in Afghanistan, covering most of the country's thirty-four provinces. Twelve PRTs are U.S.-led; fourteen are directed by other nations. Although PRT work is mostly nonmilitary in nature, a dearth of available civilian personnel means that the teams are composed primarily of military officers; of the 50 to 100 people in any given U.S.-led PRT, only three or four typically have been U.S. government civilians or contractors.[30] Some PRTs run by other countries, such as the British and Canadian teams in Helmand and Kandahar, are larger and better balanced between military and civilian personnel.

Despite these efforts, life remains very tough for the typical Afghan. An estimated 42 percent of the population still lives below the poverty line (defined as a monthly income of $14 or less), while an additional 20 percent lives only slightly above it. Only about 23 percent of the population has regular access to potable water, and in 2009 just 12 percent had access to adequate sanitation. Only one-fifth of the total Afghan population has had even limited access to electricity from the public grid.

So the situation is mixed. Security is mediocre and getting worse; the economy is poor even if it is gradually improving. The Afghan people remain more supportive of their own government and NATO than of the Taliban, but their frustration with the former is eroding their support—and helping the latter grow in strength. Support for NATO gradually declined, reaching a low of about 30 percent in early 2009. President Obama rightly realized that it was high time to get on with a new strategy. His renewed efforts on the U.S. side, and perhaps the excitement generated, at least initially, by the presidential campaign in Afghanistan, sparked a sense of optimism in Afghanistan, with polls showing an improvement in American popularity to about 60 percent by mid-summer of 2009. Taken together, these trends suggest that President Karzai plus the international community now have perhaps one last chance to make headway before much of the country is lost to the Taliban and before the population sours permanently on its own government and NATO.

Afghanistan and Its Neighbors

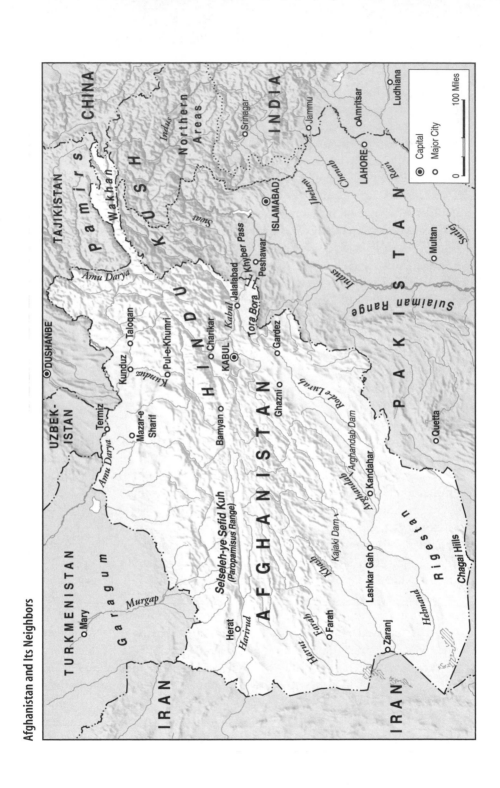

CHAPTER THREE

The Strategy

As of early 2010, by our reckoning, Afghanistan will have surpassed Vietnam as America's longest war. Surely those who call the war a quagmire would seem to have a point?

Some would counsel continued patience, offering arguments such as "the United States and its allies simply must win in Afghanistan," or "counterinsurgencies often take a decade or more to succeed," or "NATO is the most powerful alliance in history and has never lost a war," or "we cannot lose the war unless we lose our political will at home." But these exhortations, however true at one level, amount to cheerleading, not strategy.

In fact, we *could* lose in Afghanistan. Had we stayed with the strategy used during the war's first seven years, we probably would have lost. Had the strategy not changed, Afghanistan could have been torn apart, and NATO gradually demoralized to the point of giving up, by a combination of Afghan Taliban fighters; militia leaders like Gulbuddin Hekmatyar, Jalaluddin Haqqani, Anwar ul-Haq, Saifullah Mansoor, and Yunus Khalis; drug lords and other criminals; al Qaeda elements; corrupt officials; and angry Pashtun tribes.[1] These various militias and factions hardly agree on what should replace the current government, but most are agreed on the goal of defeating the new Afghan democracy and driving NATO away. They are relatively effective in cooperating, or just informally joining their efforts (with the Taliban most active in the south, the Haqqani group in the center, and Hekmatyar's Hezb-i-Islami in the northern parts of the Afghanistan-Pakistan border regions).[2]

Under the new strategy that has been taking shape since early 2009, the situation is beginning to improve. Using official documents, historical analogies, core principles of counterinsurgency, and our own analyses and observations, this chapter explains the current strategy of the foreign coalition and to a considerable extent at least of the Afghan government for trying to win this war. Most of that strategy is fairly sound, but to succeed, the strategy will have to improve further and evolve with the course of events.

WHAT IS SUCCESS?

Any evaluation of this strategy should begin with an understanding of the goal. What are we trying to accomplish in Afghanistan, at the simplest and most fundamental level? From a narrowly American point of view, the core interests are twofold: preventing a major terrorist attack that could originate on Afghan soil; and preventing instability within Afghanistan from spilling over into Pakistan, where it could threaten a much larger country possessing dozens of nuclear weapons.

Some have argued for a strategy based on counterterrorism, fought narrowly and minimally, but this approach will not work. It would quickly lose the Afghan intelligence sources, as well as the airbases for carrying out prompt attacks against extremists from unmanned aerial vehicles, that are so important for achieving both objectives. As a result, even to achieve fairly limited counterterrorism goals, we have little choice but to attempt a broader counterinsurgency strategy.

This conclusion means that we are left with the task of stabilizing Afghanistan—or at least, of giving that country and its people the tools to gradually do the stabilizing themselves. The international community and Afghan people need to build an Afghan state that is cohesive enough to control its territory, protect its population, and help its people improve their lives so that the insurgency does not resume in the future. Violence, the drug trade, and poverty need not be decisively defeated all at once to attain these basic goals. It would be enough that the country stop sliding into worsening violence and that the beginnings of a viable, legal economy begin to take root. Over time, these positive trends could be built on and strengthened, with a far smaller role for the United States and other outside powers. That is the basic concept of success we should have in mind.

American rhetoric has confused the matter of late. American officials briefed President Obama just after his inauguration about the goals of the mission in Afghanistan, and the list contained seventeen core objectives. Mr. Obama rightly realized that this was far too many. He also may have wanted to distinguish his approach from President Bush's enthusiastic promotion of democracy, a time-tested ideal of American foreign policy but one that became entangled with Mr. Bush's doctrine of preemption and his perceived tendency toward unilateralism.

President Obama settled on the core goal of defeating al Qaeda throughout the Afghanistan-Pakistan theater because that seemed the essential requirement for protecting American national security.[3] He reaffirmed that goal in his December 1 speech at West Point, where he also showed little enthusiasm for nation building in Afghanistan. But, in fact, state building at least is important, as is the degradation of the Taliban. Al Qaeda and the Taliban are increasingly intertwined by ideology, by tactical cooperation, by marriages, by colocation.[4] So defeating the Taliban is important too. And that means helping build a strong enough Afghan state that it can ultimately contain the resistance on its own. Moreover, as noted before, finding and defeating al Qaeda requires intelligence that cannot be obtained without a cooperative population, as well as bases for commandos and unmanned aerial vehicles that cannot be sustained if the Afghan government falls to the insurgents.[5]

As observed by Sarah Chayes, an extremely astute American who moved to Afghanistan several years ago to help in its reconstruction, minimalist language about our goals makes the Afghans again fear that we are not truly serious about helping them build a self-sustaining state. That in turn reduces their incentives to cooperate with us even in the counterterrorism effort, because providing intelligence and other help is risky to them—especially if we do not help give them the tools to protect themselves against the resulting backlash and reprisal attacks by insurgents.

President Obama's words that we do not seek to "rebuild Afghanistan into a Jeffersonian democracy" and Secretary Gates's statement in congressional testimony early in 2009 that we do not seek "some sort of Central Asian Valhalla over there" are of course literally true at one level. But they also risk sending a message of disinterest in the ultimate fate of the country.[6] The same message is heard in Pakistan and may persuade elements of the Inter-Services Intelligence Directorate to sustain their support for the Afghan Taliban as a hedge against premature American-NATO withdrawal.

Those seeking to distinguish the new approach from Mr. Bush's should be careful, because there is no obvious alternative to promoting democracy if we seek a stable Afghanistan. It is not as if there is a benign strongman waiting in the wings who would be widely acceptable to Afghans, and capable of running a reasonable autocracy, if only we would endorse the approach and help install the ruler. George Bush's goals were not wrong at their core; the problem was that Mr. Bush's administration did not provide adequate resources to achieve them.

All that said, Mr. Obama's actions speak louder than his words. His strategy is in fact based on the concepts of counterinsurgency, stabilization, and capacity building for Afghanistan that stand a much better chance of success than the now-discredited approaches of narrow counterterrorism tried already this decade. So despite the rhetorical confusion, things are in fact moving in the right direction.

PROTECTING THE POPULATION WHILE BUILDING UP THE GOVERNMENT

So how can we build an Afghanistan that is cohesive and controlled by its own government? If that is the ultimate goal, what are the focal points for getting there, the main priorities in the effort to help get the country on its own feet?

Two key themes should guide our efforts—protection of the Afghan population, and development of Afghan institutions capable of doing that same job themselves. Meanwhile, key populations must remain supportive of the effort—in Afghanistan certainly, and in troop-providing nations like the United States. They will likely stay supportive if they see progress in security, and in building up the Afghan army and police. Progress in people's economic situations and human rights may also help and are obviously important—but they are probably not quite as crucial to the success of the core strategy in the short term, except as they impinge directly on security.

These are ambitious goals, to be sure, but they are also finite and somewhat specific. The task before us is very difficult, but it does not require a sweeping transformation of all aspects of Afghanistan to be successful. Together these goals constitute a potential war-winning strategy for the coalition, and an exit strategy for NATO. Achieving them will not mean the end of challenges for the Afghan people and government—but it will mean that the foreign role can become much more modest, and more typical of how we interact with other countries around the world.

The first goal requires a population-focused counterinsurgency strategy. That means patrolling; policing; protecting threatened individuals; gaining people's trust; asking for their help in tracking down criminals, terrorists, and insurgents; and otherwise protecting their communities. It also means protecting key elements of economic and social life—roads, utilities, schools, hospitals, gathering places. And it means talking to and working with local leaders from the start of operations—the reason why Marine Corps Brigadier General Larry Nicholson insisted in the summer of 2009 that his company commanders have a shura meeting with local elders within twenty-four hours of arriving in a new community.[7]

This overall philosophy is distinct, and much different, from the goal of pursuing terrorists directly. The latter is what Defense Secretary Rumsfeld tried to do in the war's early years (in both Iraq and Afghanistan, in fact), minimizing our efforts at nation building and population protection in the process. President Obama was therefore potentially misleading in describing counterterrorism as the centerpiece of his new approach. But the chief elements of the new Obama plan, and many of the other words used to describe it, make clear that he is essentially pursuing counterterrorism goals with a counterinsurgency strategy. That is the right way to go, so long as it is properly resourced and properly complemented by the efforts of Afghans themselves.

The second priority of the new strategy is to help build up Afghan institutions so that, over time, they can take over the job now being done largely by outside forces. This buildup begins with training, mentoring, and partnering the Afghan security forces. Training means basic development of skills in the classroom and on weapons ranges and exercise fields; mentoring means embedding Western officers and noncommissioned officers with Afghan units when they are actually on the job; partnering means having Afghan and Western units pair up and work together in the field. All are important.

Institution building goes beyond the security forces, however, to include helping improve court systems, local governance, and the economy. Not all of these ambitious goals need to be fully achieved for the mission to succeed and for NATO ultimately to leave Afghanistan. But they should all be pursued, since it is not easy to predict which efforts will work best. Creating law and order is paramount, but some degree of economic progress, including job creation and strengthening of the legitimate agricultural economy, is also needed. The latter will to some extent flow naturally from the former.

So the concept for success, and for NATO's exit strategy, is simple to state—protect the population, build up Afghan institutions, and gradually transfer more and more responsibility to Afghans as conditions allow. It is best not to set this process to an exact calendar, because that gives too much information to enemy forces and presupposes that we can precisely schedule a complex series of events.[8] Some fault President Obama for specifying that the transfer of responsibility to Afghans and reduction in U.S. forces would begin by July 2011, but administration officials were clear that the pace of these changes would be "conditions-based." Our best forecast, given the rate at which NATO will be able to help Afghans build up their institutions, is that substantial NATO forces will have to be in the country for five to seven more years. If the strategy works as intended—if enough resources are deployed to key parts of the country, and enough Afghan security forces as well as other parts of government are better trained and mentored, we should see major progress by 2010 or early 2011, as discussed further in chapter 5.

How do these various ideas and priorities for the mission affect the issue of counternarcotics in Afghanistan? Even the more ambitious plans for crop substitution being tried promise only a 50 percent reduction in opium production over a five- to eight-year period.[9] If we had to wipe out most of the drug trade to succeed in this war, such realities would be daunting. Admittedly, illicit drugs are a huge problem for Afghanistan, and they also help fund the insurgents—to the tune of perhaps $70 million to $100 million a year, although figures are imprecise of course, and in any event the Taliban has numerous other sources of revenue such as demanding "taxes" or protection money from local inhabitants or businesses, kidnapping for ransom, and receiving money from extremists abroad.[10] But we need not eliminate the opium trade to arrest the worsening tide of violence; gradual reductions in the poppy business will probably suffice, when combined with other efforts, including ongoing help for the Afghan economy.

Counterinsurgency theorists like to use the slogan "clear, hold, build."[11] These words describe the sequential steps counterinsurgency forces attempt to take to win back a given village, town, city, or broader region from insurgent forces. The idea is that insurgents and terrorists must be rooted out, in the clearing or offensive phase. Next, enough policing and other fighting capability must be retained to prevent insurgents from returning—the "hold" phase. Finally, indigenous institutions must be built up so that the local population has incentives to cooperate with government forces and oppose the insurgency over the long term. Some administration officials now add "transfer" as a fourth step, but this is, in fact, an inherent part of the building process.

Counterinsurgency missions are troop intensive because so much protection of the population is involved. That does not literally mean guarding individuals, except when specific persons are known to be at heightened risk of attack. Rather, it means having enough presence on the ground to understand the relationships among locals in a given area and to build trust with civilians who will usually be the best sources of intelligence on enemy activity. That means returning to given neighborhoods and streets often enough to create a feeling of confidence among locals and to deter crime—or, failing that, punish it quickly even when it is not successfully prevented. It is because of personnel demands like these that the U.S. military's *Counterinsurgency Manual* estimates that successful counterinsurgencies require roughly twenty to twenty-five troops or police for every 1,000 citizens.[12] The manual, written in 2006 under the guidance of then–lieutenant generals David Petraeus (U.S. Army) and James Amos (U.S. Marine Corps), also discusses the necessary nonmilitary aspects of policy, including improved governance and economic development.[13]

OBAMA'S STRATEGY

Most of these principles are general truths about successful counterinsurgency, some of which were being applied in Afghanistan even before Obama's presidency. In fact, Defense Secretary Gates was promising more U.S. troops for the war even in the summer of 2008, and General David McKiernan—before being replaced by General Stanley McChrystal as commander of the mission—was developing a new strategy for Afghanistan seeking to establish better control of certain contested areas of the country.

But President Obama had to do more than voice general principles; he needed to make concrete decisions about how many forces to send, how many more civilian experts to deploy, how much extra aid money to provide, and what additional allied assistance to request from NATO and other key players. He decided in March 2009 to increase the U.S. military capability in Afghanistan to 68,000 uniformed personnel for an indefinite period, with the possibility of further increases thereafter. His December 1 speech will now push that number to 100,000.[14]

It is worth excerpting from Obama's speech of March 27, 2009, to understand some of the key elements of this new plan:

> I've already ordered the deployment of 17,000 troops that had been requested by General McKiernan for many months. These soldiers and Marines will take the fight to the Taliban in the south and the east, and give us a greater capacity to partner with Afghan security forces and to go after insurgents along the border. This push will also help provide security in advance of the important presidential elections in Afghanistan in August. At the same time, we will shift the emphasis of our mission to training and increasing the size of Afghan security forces, so that they can eventually take the lead in securing their country. That's how we will prepare Afghans to take responsibility for their security, and how we will ultimately be able to bring our own troops home.
>
> For three years, our commanders have been clear about the resources they need for training. And those resources have been denied because of the war in Iraq. Now, that will change. The additional troops that we deployed have already increased our training capacity. And later this spring we will deploy approximately 4,000 U.S. troops to train Afghan security forces. For the first time, this will truly resource our effort to train and support the Afghan army and police. Every American unit in Afghanistan will be partnered with an Afghan unit, and we will seek additional trainers from our NATO allies to ensure that every Afghan unit has a coalition partner. We will accelerate our efforts to build an Afghan army of 134,000 and a police force of 82,000 so that we can meet these goals by 2011—and increases in Afghan forces may very well be needed as our plans to turn over security responsibility to the Afghans go forward.
>
> This push must be joined by a dramatic increase in our civilian effort. Afghanistan has an elected government, but it is undermined by corruption and has difficulty delivering basic services to its

people. The economy is undercut by a booming narcotics trade that encourages criminality and funds the insurgency. . . .

So to advance security, opportunity and justice—not just in Kabul, but from the bottom up in the provinces—we need agricultural specialists and educators, engineers and lawyers. That's how we can help the Afghan government serve its people and develop an economy that isn't dominated by illicit drugs. And that's why I'm ordering a substantial increase in our civilians on the ground. That's also why we must seek civilian support from our partners and allies, from the United Nations and international aid organizations—an effort that Secretary [of State Hillary Rodham] Clinton will carry forward next week in The Hague. . . .

As we provide these resources, the days of unaccountable spending, no-bid contracts, and wasteful reconstruction must end. So my budget will increase funding for a strong Inspector General at both the State Department and USAID [U.S. Agency for International Development], and include robust funding for the special inspector generals for Afghan Reconstruction.

And I want to be clear: We cannot turn a blind eye to the corruption that causes Afghans to lose faith in their own leaders. Instead, we will seek a new compact with the Afghan government that cracks down on corrupt behavior, and sets clear benchmarks, clear metrics for international assistance so that it is used to provide for the needs of the Afghan people

In a country with extreme poverty that's been at war for decades, there will also be no peace without reconciliation among former enemies. Now, I have no illusion that this will be easy. In Iraq, we had success in reaching out to former adversaries to isolate and target al Qaeda in Iraq. We must pursue a similar process in Afghanistan, while understanding that it is a very different country.

There is an uncompromising core of the Taliban. They must be met with force, and they must be defeated. But there are also those who've taken up arms because of coercion, or simply for a price. These Afghans must have the option to choose a different course. And that's why we will work with local leaders, the Afghan government, and international partners to have a reconciliation process in every province. As their ranks dwindle, an enemy that has nothing to offer the Afghan people but terror and repression must be further isolated. And we will continue to support the basic human rights of all Afghans—including women and girls.

My administration is committed to strengthening international organizations and collective action. . . . As America does more, we will ask others to join us in doing their part. From our partners and NATO allies, we will seek not simply troops, but rather clearly defined capabilities: supporting the Afghan elections, training Afghan security forces, a greater civilian commitment to the Afghan people. For the United Nations, we seek greater progress for its mandate to coordinate international action and assistance, and to strengthen Afghan institutions.

And finally, together with the United Nations, we will forge a new Contact Group for Afghanistan and Pakistan that brings together all who should have a stake in the security of the region— our NATO allies and other partners, but also the Central Asian states, the Gulf nations and Iran; Russia, India and China. None of these nations benefit from a base for al Qaeda terrorists, and a region that descends into chaos. All have a stake in the promise of lasting peace and security and development. [15]

President Obama's December 2009 speech voiced many similar themes, as he approved the addition of another 30,000 American troops for the mission, as well as ongoing American economic aid. Yet he also sent a clear message to Afghan president Karzai that corruption needed to be reduced. Karzai's government has welcomed Obama's speech and promised to address the criticisms about corruption.

FROM OBAMA'S STRATEGY TO MCCHRYSTAL'S OPERATIONAL PLAN

Of course, it is not just a question of how many troops will be in Afghanistan, but where they will be deployed and what they will do. In broad brush, under Obama's strategy the United States will lead a strong NATO effort to reinforce the south and east of Afghanistan, areas where the Pashtun-dominated enemy is strongest and the fighting heaviest.

More specifically, by late 2009 the United States had deployed what amounted to a "3 + 3 + 2" plan: roughly three brigades in the east, three more in the south, and two more dedicated to training Afghan security forces. (Each Army brigade has about 3,500 soldiers plus support units that typically at least double the overall effective size of the brigade.) These troops are working with roughly a brigade and a half of additional NATO forces in both east and south as well. The forces added during Obama's first year include a combat aviation brigade and a "Stryker brigade" (built around a medium-weight combat vehicle of that same name) for Kandahar Province and a Marine Expeditionary Brigade (with associated airpower of its own) for Helmand Province. Finally the fourth brigade of the 82nd Airborne Division joined the existing 48th National Guard brigade with the Combined Security Transition Command–Afghanistan to train Afghan security forces. At most points before 2008, virtually no U.S. forces were in southern Afghanistan; it is also significant that the combat aviation brigade roughly quintuples the airpower available in that vicinity.[16] Additional forces approved on December 1, 2009, include two more U.S. brigades for the south and one more for the east, probably, as well as another training brigade to be spread to several areas.

The added forces are being used to secure major highways in the country and to expand coverage of populated regions. The exact approaches vary from place to place. In Kandahar, for example, the idea is to keep large numbers of U.S. and Canadian troops out of Kandahar City proper out of concern that a big Western presence could stoke opposition. Limited numbers of NATO soldiers will establish joint stations with Afghans within the city. Other reinforcements will deploy along the transportation arteries leading into the city.[17]

Unlike Iraq, a more urban country with hundreds of unoccupied buildings at the start of the surge (a result of the sectarian cleansing that had occurred by then), much of Afghanistan is rural, and virtually all buildings are overcrowded. Thus, securing village populations will typically not mean moving NATO forces into vacant buildings but rather building small encampments near villages, ideally on high ground overlooking both the village and access points to it.[18]

As the new forces have deployed, they have worked their way into the field, first establishing battalion lodgments and then gradually setting up forward bases for companies and even platoons. A central question has been "how low can we go?" in terms of the size of the units that are forward deployed. Deploying Western forces in smaller groups than 50 to 100 is generally not realistic. For one thing, the insurgents have shown the ability to mass up to 200 fighters at a time; for another, to be able to protect itself, any forward outpost should have a range of capabilities, including medical and logistics personnel.[19]

Afghanistan has more than 25,000 villages, with perhaps 10,000 in the crucial south and east, so a Western force that totals about 140,000 will never be able to protect all, or even most, of them. McChrystal is choosing to focus on the larger towns and cities, the key population centers, and the strategic areas near highways and main river valleys.

Some analysts are hoping that the additional forces will help reduce the flow of insurgents into the country from Pakistan. The military already undertakes actions to slow that flow, ambushing known infiltration routes and manning checkpoints and patrols on highways, often in collaboration with Afghan security forces.[20] But because most of the Afghan resistance is believed to be local, according to McChrystal's August 2009 strategic assessment, this mission will not receive primary emphasis.[21] Moreover, McChrystal has chosen to focus more on population centers and less on remote border areas.[22]

Perhaps most important of all, many of the additional U.S. forces will be used to train the Afghan military and police forces. Going beyond what was done in Iraq, McChrystal emphasizes not only good initial training for Afghan forces and the embedding of mentoring teams within army and police units thereafter, but also a formal partnering between Afghan and NATO units, where they would pair off as "sister formations" and train, plan, deploy, patrol, and fight together. This apprenticeship concept is similar to an approach that Senator Carl Levin of the Senate Armed Services Committee and some other members of Congress have promoted. A key difference, however, is that Levin sees partnering as a way to reduce demands on U.S. forces, whereas McChrystal does not. In fact his fall 2009 request for more Western forces derives largely from this partnering concept.

According to McChrystal the goal of this sister-unit pairing concept is to build up Afghanistan security forces to be larger and more effective—ultimately reaching levels of 240,000 Afghan soldiers and 160,000 police.[23] President Obama declined to endorse these goals, but instead will aim for the interim levels of 134,000 army and 96,000 police by late 2010, and then reassess. Over time a smaller NATO unit might be able to partner with a larger Afghan one—say, a NATO battalion (of about 800 troops) for an Afghan brigade (of some 2,000 to 3,000). But at first, given the current lack of adequate Afghan forces, the NATO and Afghan units would likely be of comparable size.[24]

Several other elements of the evolving Afghanistan strategy are worth noting. As McChrystal assumed command in June 2009, he was granted first dibs on personnel who would become part of an ongoing Afghanistan experts group within the military—even when they are back in the United States on rotation. The idea is to develop more continuity and expertise in the country.

McChrystal is also creating stronger "fusion" centers, where different types of intelligence are shared, provided quickly to operational planners, and made available to allies as well. As a result, more effective commando and air attacks on specific leadership targets were already being carried out by late 2009, because actionable intelligence could be cross-checked and verified more quickly than before, allowing Afghan and coalition forces to strike before they lost sight of key battlefield adversaries. The strike teams have been strengthened, too. The overall intelligence effort now focuses much more than it did in the past on understanding the "human terrain"—the constellation of tribes and other key actors in a given area, both potential allies and potential or actual adversaries. This was clear to one of us (O'Hanlon) on a trip to southern Afghanistan in November 2009, where coalition units had in effect created anthropology cells to study local tribes, and where top battlefield commanders considered understanding tribal dynamics to be among their top priorities.

In addition, the selection of General McChrystal as the commander of all U.S. units in country as well as NATO's International Security Assistance Force (ISAF) coincided with a decision, formally effective as of September 2009, to create a three-star command position to maintain operational control of all forces in country. An American officer and Afghanistan combat veteran, Lieutenant General David Rodriguez, was assigned this intermediate joint command position with NATO approval. The idea is to have Rodriguez focus on the myriad day-to-day decisions about deploying and operating forces, while McChyrstal directs his primary attention to broader strategic matters, including integration with civilian efforts. The idea builds on a similar concept employed in Iraq and makes eminent sense.

Another key concept is to build on the success of Marine Major General Douglas Stone in Iraq, who revolutionized prison policy there. The goal is to handle detainees much more carefully so that detention facilities in Afghanistan do not become the equivalent of "terrorist universities" as sometimes happened earlier in both Iraq and Afghanistan. According to McChrystal's summer 2009 strategic assessment, the Afghan Corrections System holds almost 15,000 inmates—but perhaps just over 2,500 are Taliban and al Qaeda, the rest being common criminals of one stripe or another.[25] Holding thieves and others guilty of relatively minor infractions in the same facilities as committed terrorists and insurgents greatly increases the risks that the common criminals will be converted to extremist views. It is important to separate the "reconciliables" from the "irreconciliables," giving minor criminals job training and releasing them as quickly as possible.[26] McChrystal's strategic assessment underscores the need to give Afghanistan the lead role in incarcerating and handling detainees, while making it possible for ISAF to conduct interviews and interrogations as needed.[27] A new detention facility at Bagram airfield north of Kabul has just opened with these priorities in mind.[28]

As noted earlier, the role of offensive power in general and air strikes in particular is a crucial aspect of the NATO approach. Offensive missions must be careful to target only the enemy as much as possible and not hurt civilians inadvertently. This is not only a moral issue but a practical, strategic one; accidental killings of innocents breed more angry Afghans and thus more insurgents (Sarah Chayes suggests that we assume there will be three to five new recruits for the Taliban for every innocent killed). Here, NATO has been remiss for much of the war, with its own bombs and other weapons killing anywhere from 20 to 40 percent of the Afghan civilians who have perished in the violence. The fact that NATO's intentions are good, and that insurgent forces usually draw fire from NATO—often with the explicit goal of having foreign forces cause civilian fatalities inadvertently—is no excuse. McChrystal's decision to be more restrictive in the use of airpower led to nearly a 50 percent reduction in the use of air ordnance in the summer of 2009 relative to the summer of 2008, and significant declines in Afghan casualties as well.[29]

McChrystal's directives to avoid using heavy ground weapons in situations where civilians could be hurt, except to save the lives of troops in contact, are a further wise recognition of the damage civilian casualties can cause to Afghan support for the mission. In fact, he has even told troops to break off firefights rather than risk harm to innocents.[30] He also wants to avoid having ISAF convoys push Afghans off roads and is similarly refining normal operational procedures in other ways to send a message of greater solidarity with the Afghan people. To set the right tone and send the right message, McChrystal himself tries to avoid using body armor and to limit the size of his own security detail when visiting Afghans.[31]

Using greater care—and having more ground forces with many more helicopters available for rapid reaction in the future—will not prevent tragic accidents. But these new approaches can, and must, reduce the dependence on firepower and the resulting political fallout.[32] So will an approach that General Petraeus calls "being first with the truth"—not only acknowledging forthrightly when things go badly but also explaining the context and causes of any tragedy and the steps being taken to reduce similar mishaps in the future.[33]

Of course huge challenges remain for NATO, starting with the fact that for the first seven years of the war, Western forces lost ground. The insurgency expanded; many Afghan reformers were killed, driven away, or otherwise discouraged; and many "fence-sitters" among the population joined, or at least condoned or tolerated, insurgent forces out of frustration. General McChrystal's forces do not yet have the full knowledge of the local population that they need to figure out how to motivate various tribes to work with them rather than against them. They do not have a viable Afghan government in place as a partner, and the international aid effort is uncoordinated and often weak as well. After areas are cleared, the building phase is slow to start as a result. McChrystal and other leaders are making impressive gains given their room to maneuver—but that room to maneuver is often limited.

OBAMA'S SECOND REVIEW—AND SECOND TROOP INCREASE

General McChrystal arrived in Kabul in June 2009. As requested by Secretary Gates, he then proceeded to carry out a sixty-day assessment of conditions in the country as he saw them, followed by any adjustments to strategy and any requests for additional resources that he might be inclined to propose.

McChrystal's subsequent request for four more combat brigades and a total of 40,000 additional troops, formally presented to the White House late in the summer of 2009, was based on his team's assessment of how many troops would be needed to carry out his strategy systematically. McChrystal's goal is to apply his approach, not nationwide, but principally in the south and east of the country, and in the most populous regions. In fact, even as U.S. forces increase further under his strategy, the number of districts in which NATO forces normally operate is expected to decline somewhat, to about 80 of the country's nearly 400. So the approach is discriminating. Yet at the same time it is thorough, seeking to establish a contiguous zone of safety throughout the country's crucial south and east, where the population can feel relatively secure, transportation can take place reliably, and Afghan institutions can take root. Until now, even where NATO forces have been able to clear and hold, as in roughly two-thirds of populated parts of Helmand Province, they have not been able to consolidate such zones. As a result insurgents retain local sanctuaries from which to strike out. A case in point is in central Helmand, where as of late 2009 the town of Nawa had been cleared and largely secured but where the nearby town of Marja remained in unfriendly hands. As a result, assassination attempts against reformist officials in Nawa were being attempted out of Marja.

As noted, and in response, the McChrystal plan reportedly seeks to place initial reinforcements in the south of the country (the first two brigades). The third brigade would then go to the east, while any parts of a fourth provided by allies would be held in operational reserve (perhaps for use in the increasingly troubled north and west, with some eventual U.S. help).[34] President Obama approved 30,000 added American troops in response to General McChrystal's analysis.

An assessment like McChrystal's 2009 effort had not previously been done. McKiernan's earlier troop request, and Obama's March 2009 authorization for additional forces, sought to add U.S. units where the situation had deteriorated. These were essentially defensive reactions, even if far more muscular than policy had been to date. McChrystal's plan, by contrast, is based on first principles of counterinsurgency and seeks to establish the initiative for Afghan and NATO forces rather than simply react to problems as they develop. It also seeks to create conditions where more Afghan elders and tribal leaders will begin to do what has started in Helmand—recommend their own tribal sons for positions in the Afghan security forces. The NATO presence gives them the confidence that such recommendations are not a death warrant for their youth, because Afghan units will work so closely with NATO forces under the McChrystal approach. As such initiatives gain momentum, and pay and survivors' benefits are increased for the police and army as well, service becomes more appealing. That is the theory, and it already shows some signs of proving out.

At a tactical military level, it is hard to disagree with McChrystal's call for additional troops. Even with Obama's initial increases, total Afghan-NATO-U.S. forces in the country remained woefully short of what General Petraeus and General Amos's 2006 counterinsurgency manual would suggest. For a population of 30 million, their methodology implies the need for 600,000 counterinsurgents; however, the NATO-led foreign coalition presumably will have only about 140,000 troops, and Afghanistan forces between 200,000 and 300,000 over the 2010–11 period.

But this shortfall should be acceptable. The Amos-Petraeus guidelines are approximations based on historical experience, not hard and fast laws of physics. Moreover, much of northern and western Afghanistan today resembles a peacekeeping mission more than a hard-core counterinsurgency. It is worth bearing in mind that in Afghanistan, 70 percent of the violence occurs in 10 percent of the country.[35] To be sure, the remaining 30 percent of the violence is not insignificant, and the enemy could also redirect its effort to some extent in response to the new strategy. However, the unfriendliness of most of the country to the Taliban movement will limit its ability to do so. So the planned number of forces may suffice.

The additional troops will be mostly American, at least at first. Most other NATO countries are uninterested in adding large numbers of troops to the mission, and in fact the Netherlands and Canada plan to pull out their forces fairly soon. But Obama may convince allies to add some 5,000 to 7,000 more troops, meaning that McChrystal will get at least 35,000 of the 40,000 total added forces he recommended. Perhaps we could ask Muslim allies such as Morocco and Indonesia to deploy troops.[36] But the main needs are now in the south and east, and the list of countries volunteering to add capability in these places—or even sustain current commitments—is quite short.

THE PAKISTAN DIMENSION

The role of Pakistan is crucial in the Afghan war, as well as in the broader war on terrorism. It is there that al Qaeda leadership has had its redoubts in recent years (most likely in the Federally Administered Tribal Areas); it is there that the Afghan Taliban movement has its headquarters; it is there that the stakes are also inherently highest, given Pakistan's large size and its possession of a nuclear arsenal that must never be allowed to fall into extremist hands. The year 2009 was relatively

Northern Region of the Afghanistan-Pakistan Border

Central Region of the Afghanistan-Pakistan Border

Southern Region of the Afghanistan-Pakistan Border

encouraging in some ways, with the government assertively moving against Pakistani Taliban in the Swat Valley and South Waziristan even in the face of multiple suicide bombings and other attacks from the resistance. But it remains to be seen if Pakistan's commitment will continue, and if it will be willing to take any steps against the Afghan Taliban—a group largely distinct from, if related to, the foe it faces internally on its own territory.

The Obama administration has recognized the stakes here. Beyond his specific plans for Afghanistan, President Obama proposed roughly tripling economic aid to Pakistan, to about $1.5 billion a year. Congress has now passed and funded this request (originally sponsored in part by then-Senator Biden). Despite some Pakistani objections that the United States was imposing too many conditions on the aid, and had too many requirements for certification of Pakistan's progress in pursuing extremists, the legislation is still a positive step forward. General Petraeus also proposed a further military aid package for Pakistan that would supplement previous assistance with another $3 billion over five years focused on counterinsurgency training and equipment—such as helicopters and night vision technology—for the Pakistani army and Frontier Corps.[37] Total security-related aid from the United States to Pakistan is now roughly another $1.5 billion a year.

Some additional aspects of administration policy toward Pakistan can be gleaned from excerpts of a white paper released at the time Obama delivered his March 2009 speech. The policy paper outlined the uses of additional aid as well as the challenges of working with Pakistan at a time when its willingness to pursue extremists on its own soil has at times been shaky:

Bolstering Afghanistan-Pakistan cooperation
    We need to institutionalize stronger mechanisms for bilateral and trilateral cooperation. During the process of this review, interagency teams from Afghanistan and Pakistan came to Washington, D.C., for trilateral meetings. This new forum should continue and serve as the basis for enhanced bilateral and trilateral cooperation.
Engaging and focusing Islamabad on the common threat
    Successfully shutting down the Pakistani safe haven for extremists will also require consistent and intensive strategic engagement with Pakistani leadership in both the civilian and military spheres. The engagement must be conducted in a way that respects, and indeed enhances, democratic civilian authority.

Assisting Pakistan's capability to fight extremists

It is vital to strengthen our efforts to both develop and operationally enable Pakistani security forces so they are capable of succeeding in sustained counterterrorism and counterinsurgency operations. In part this will include increased U.S. military assistance for helicopters to provide air mobility, night vision equipment, and training and equipment specifically for Pakistani Special Operation Forces and their Frontier Corps.

Increasing and broadening assistance in Pakistan

Increasing economic assistance to Pakistan—to include direct budget support, development assistance, infrastructure investment, and technical advice on making sound economic policy adjustments—and strengthening trade relations will maximize support for our policy aims; it should also help to provide longer-term economic stability. Our assistance should focus on long-term capacity building, on agricultural sector job creation, education and training, and on infrastructure requirements. Assistance should also support Pakistani efforts to "hold and build" in western Pakistan as a part of its counterinsurgency efforts.

Exploring other areas of economic cooperation with Pakistan

We need to enhance bilateral and regional trade possibilities, in part through implementing Reconstruction Opportunity Zones (which were recently reintroduced in Congress) and encouraging foreign investment in key sectors, such as energy. In addition, assisting Islamabad with developing a concrete strategy for utilizing donor aid would increase Islamabad's chances for garnering additional support from the international community.[38]

WRESTLING WITH THE CORRUPTION ISSUE

Some criticized President Obama for taking three months to review his options in the fall of 2009, after receiving General McChrystal's assessment of battlefield conditions and the state of Afghanistan more generally. However, the president's patient approach was understandable. For starters, in early 2009 military leaders told Mr. Obama that perhaps a total of 70,000 to 80,000 U.S. troops would be enough to implement a major new strategy, and he gave them most of what they wanted. Subsequently, as a result of the McChrystal assessment, they said that they needed more than 100,000 GIs for essentially the same strategy. We do not fault them; these kinds of military judgments are inherently imprecise. But Mr. Obama was entitled to think twice about their methods for determining force requirements under the circumstances. Yes, the field commander had changed in the interim, but he was changed at the initial recommendation of the Pentagon, not the White House, which had reasonable grounds to be a little skeptical about why troop requirements had escalated so dramatically.

The most crucial point, however, is this: the war cannot be won without a viable Afghan government. Even if NATO started doing everything right, President Karzai needs to improve his performance. He made a good start with his decision to agree to a runoff election for the presidency (even though it ultimately proved unnecessary), after initially resisting the idea when it became clear that he had not secured the requisite 50 percent in the August 20, 2009, round. His decision was reportedly facilitated by arguments from Ambassador Eikenberry, Senator John Kerry, and others that the United States would not be able to maintain a strong partnership with Afghanistan absent a reasonably legitimate election process. Deferring any decision on a troop increase made this argument more credible.

With the election behind him, Karzai must now follow up with a serious anticorruption plan. Miracles are not possible. But neither are they necessary. A reasonable degree of progress is enough to make a big difference. Karzai needs to fire the worst of the worst among his corrupt cohorts, find more credible means of awarding construction contracts so that they are not all won by businesses owned by his relatives and friends, appoint independent inspectors general within key government agencies, and create ombudsmen to allow citizens to complain when they see graft or suffer poor government services. President Obama was right to keep some leverage over Karzai, however modest it might have been, as the Afghan president made his initial decisions about how to form his new governing team and what to emphasize in his governing agenda for his second term. President Karzai has been seen as a conciliator, trying to create a big tent of many leaders, businessmen, politicians, warlords, former mujahedin, former exiles, and others to create the new Afghanistan. To some extent this has left him open to charges that he has tolerated the presence of too many bad actors, not necessarily because he is personally corrupt or directly complicit, but because he lacks firmness and resolve, and perhaps takes an overly forgiving approach in the reconciliation process.

This criticism is at least partly unfair, because initially Karzai did not have the tools to create a strong state and by necessity had to tolerate a continued role for warlords. Only now is he within sight of having a large enough army and police force to run the country in a more orderly manner. But in light of that evolution, and the clear evidence that his approach of the first term failed to stanch the deterioration of the country's security environment, he now faces a choice as he begins his second term as president. Will he be a leader who is associated with unsavory, corrupt elements? Or will he be willing to bring at least some order and sense of justice to a government increasingly seen by its own people as morally bankrupt? Karzai need not necessarily fire close associates based on past behavior, but he can serve notice that future behavior will be more closely scrutinized and do more to ensure a fairer distribution of government contracts across a wider range of individuals and companies (and tribes).

Some promising developments are already apparent on the anticorruption front. One example is in the security forces. General McChrystal's new partnering concept provides NATO forces with much more information about the performance, and dependability, of individual Afghan leaders, particularly within the army and police. Armed with such information, NATO officials can approach Afghan leaders like Minister of Interior Hanif Atmar and Minister of Defense Abdul Rahim Wardak and suggest improvements in certain leadership roles. Atmar and Wardak (or their successors, as appropriate) may consider other factors besides the NATO recommendations, of course, but by most accounts, this process is starting to work reasonably well.[39] Karzai has also appointed other good leaders; in December 8, 2009, testimony, Ambassador Eikenberry mentioned ministers of interior, finance, health, commerce, and education, as well as the Major Crimes Task Force.

AFGHAN PLANS, THE AFGHAN BUDGET, AND INTERNATIONAL AID EFFORTS

The economic program for Afghanistan also needs substantial improvement. This is not really an area of disagreement between Kabul and the outside world; rather it is an area where all have collectively fallen short of the desired performance. There has been progress, as noted—with schools and health clinics, cell phones and media, construction projects in the big cities and near the main roads, aided by the stimulus that comes from massive amounts of foreign aid dollars (not to mention the opium trade). However, Afghanistan remains extremely poor, with a GDP of not much more than $12 billion, or roughly $400 per capita, and estimates of unemployment remain around 40 percent.[40] Clearly the country has a long way to go before it can truly stand on its feet.

In 2009 (referred to as year 1388 in official Afghan documents, to reflect the number of years since 622, when the Prophet Muhammad and his followers left Mecca to settle in Medina), the Afghanistan government's total budget was equivalent to about $3 billion. Only about $1 billion of that came from Afghan sources; the rest was foreign aid of one type or another.[41]

U.S. economic aid has averaged nearly $1 billion annually in recent years.[42] Other large sources of aid are the United Kingdom, Japan, the European Union, the World Bank, and the Asian Development Bank. Some funds are pooled together before being disbursed, going into trust funds for Afghanistan reconstruction or for law and order. Others are administered by individual donors. Still others are organized into thematic efforts, such as the so-called Afghanistan Sub-National Governance Program with donors that include the European Union and the U.N. Development Program. The initiative works with relevant Afghan institutions to train officials in needed governing skills at the provincial, district, city, and village levels of government.[43]

The $3 billion total annual budget is broken into two main pieces— an operating budget of about $1.8 billion and a development budget of just over $1.1 billion. The amounts have varied over the years; in 2008, the budget was actually larger, at close to $4 billion, but not all funds were disbursed, so the 2009 figures do not really represent a reduction in the scale of effort. The operating budget, featuring recurrent annual expenses, is dominated by the ministries of defense and interior (each costing over $400 million annually). The ministry of education is third at just under $300 million. The budgets for health care and other individual categories of expenditure are each under $50 million.

The development budget is dominated by costs for infrastructure (about $450 million annually), agriculture and related rural development efforts ($280 million), education ($140 million), health ($100 million), and economic governance (also about $100 million). These outlays are organized and prioritized under what is generally known as the Afghanistan National Development Strategy. Various local efforts are organized to a large extent under the so-called National Solidarity Program, run by the Afghan Ministry of Rural Rehabilitation and Development. This program attempts to spur community organization and activism at the district and village level—among other things providing grants typically of $20,000 to $60,000 to villages that have formed Community Development Councils and together established a list of priority projects.[44] Other types of development efforts include strengthening the field activities of the national ministries, as well as helping local government officials become more effective at their jobs.

All of these efforts, and all of these donor funds and activities, are well intentioned. But they are also relatively disorganized. They have also failed to reach remote parts of the country in many cases. New efforts are now being made to form district support teams—groups of Afghans and international workers who deploy quickly to a local area soon after military operations have made it relatively safe. They are to include representatives from the Afghan ministries of agriculture, health, education, rural development, and finance. Unfortunately, these capabilities are only now being formed as of early 2010. The delays have been unpardonable, but they are now being rectified. At least there is more rapid movement on the international civilian side; as of early 2010 the United States alone will have about 100 civilians in the southern sector of the country, contrasted with fewer than 10 in late 2008. Such foreign presence is of course no substitute for Afghan governmental capacity, but it helps.

The current Afghan budget is not anything close to sustainable. On the one hand, government revenues, now only about 7 or 8 percent of GDP, should probably double over the next five years—most other less developed countries are able to collect at least 15 percent of GDP through taxes and duties.[45] And the (legal) economy should grow too. On the other hand, expenses are going to increase further as security forces grow, and as the government increases salaries for its employees so they are not all pulled away by the lure of better-paying jobs with foreign contractors and militaries, nongovernmental organizations, and businesses. So foreign assistance will need to remain robust for many years to come and in fact will have to increase.

At least there is some good news: the economy has been growing steadily, despite a slowdown in 2008 and early 2009 until a good agricultural harvest in 2009 turned things back in a brighter direction. Inflation is in check, and basic services are improving.[46] But it will take a long time to build a real economy. Consider this observation from an Afghan government document: "Exports are unlikely to increase substantially from the current very low base. Afghanistan's exports are currently dominated by low value-added agricultural exports and carpets. Scaling up the export base would require significant FDI [foreign direct investment] inflows. Under the current situation, FDI is concentrated in the telecommunications sector and the financial sector, which are not export-oriented industries. Large scale exploitation of copper, natural gas, petroleum and precious minerals will help in the medium and long term."[47] It will remain difficult to elicit the foreign investment needed to create those mineral exploitation capacities in light of current security conditions.

The country's development strategy still seeks to aid industry and agriculture where possible. A good example is irrigation. The number of hectares under irrigation has dropped from 3.3 million before 1979 to 1.8 million today. The government believes that up to 5.3 million hectares are irrigable and is working hard with donors on various dam and canal projects, among other things, to increase available irrigation. This is the sort of development project that can be fairly easily mapped out, resourced, and pursued—if security conditions, the real crux of the matter, so allow.[48]

Since President Obama came to office, movement on such fronts has picked up. As an effort to create a "civilian surge" of sorts, U.S. civilians in Afghanistan grew from about 300 in early 2009 to 600 by October, with a goal of about 1,000 for early 2010 (and with a request by Ambassador Eikenberry for another 300 on top of that). This is all very promising. Underscoring the challenge, however, only 157 of the 600 or so had deployed out of Kabul by October 2009, reflecting the difficulty of working in remote areas under current security conditions. Thankfully, the PRT concept provides one way of protecting civilians who do work in such challenging places.[49]

Aid efforts that are seen as fair and less corrupt are crucially and urgently important in Afghanistan. It should be emphasized, however, that Afghanistan's ability to pay for its own needs is not necessary anytime soon. Right now, the goal is to defeat the insurgency; some aspects of sustainable development can be pursued patiently and gradually. Even if the world community must contribute several billion dollars a year to development projects as well as to Afghan security forces indefinitely, that is a small price compared with either the costs of defeat or the added costs of trying to impose a victory through a huge ongoing Western military presence for many years.

RECONCILIATION

Many wonder if a way out of this war can be found not by defeating the enemy but by co-opting it and negotiating with it. Put that way, the idea has appeal. It also has recent validation in Iraq, where many Sunni groups in particular came to the support of the United States and the Iraqi government as part of the Awakening movement. In Afghanistan switching sides in response to shifts in battlefield momentum also has a long history. In addition, President Karzai has himself shown interest in reconciliation, attempting talks with Taliban leaders. As he put it in the summer of 2009, "I will continue this process of participation so that all Afghans have a stake in the Afghan government, so that every Afghan feels that 'I belong to this land and I am its owner and there is a place for me in its government and its society.'"[50]

While some of what President Karzai has attempted has a certain logic, we are deeply skeptical of an intensified version of this approach, at least as it is frequently discussed. Reconciliation has a role, in fact a big role, in Afghanistan. But it is much more promising to pursue reconciliation with local leaders, mullahs, and tribal chiefs than with Taliban or other militia leaders. To borrow David Kilcullen's phrase, we are much more likely to reconcile with "accidental guerrillas" than with committed ones.

To recall what may be obvious, their core ideology makes the Taliban extremely intolerant of nonbelievers. The Taliban would not only demand the immediate departure of all foreign troops but place extreme constraints on the role of women in society, impose a brutal form of sharia law to punish those who run afoul of the organization, and avoid all forms of modernization including activities ranging from immunizations for children to scientific education to open communications with the world. The Taliban have an extremely backward and severe vision for the future life of the Afghan people; they are not simply a conservative movement, and they do not have a popular following among most Afghans (who consistently give it less than 10 percent support in polls). Taliban progress in recent years has more to do with creating fear, and admittedly establishing an impressive form of discipline within its ranks, than with developing popular support. Moreover, the Quetta shura and other major resistance leaders sense the possibility of victory and are highly unlikely to reach out halfway. To be sure, there is logic in trying to negotiate with those who would soften their views and collaborate with the government—but we already have ample reason to think such individuals are very few and far between among Taliban leaders.

Given that Karzai's efforts to negotiate and reconcile with supposedly moderate elements of the Taliban have failed at the national level, it is puzzling to many Afghans that President Obama has also been talking about negotiating with "moderates."[51] A few mid-level Taliban commanders have in fact switched sides, and there is merit in exploring whether more might do so—perhaps even bringing some of their fighters along with them if they do.[52] But the numbers are likely to be small. It is also worth noting that no third party is available to play the role of common enemy as al Qaeda did with the Sons of Iraq in al-Anbar Province and elsewhere. By this point, al Qaeda and most Afghan Taliban are so intertwined that it is hard to distinguish between them—and they certainly do not fight each other on a large scale, reducing our opportunities to forge alliances with one group against the other.

Indeed, shortly after Mr. Obama raised the subject of reconciliation in early 2009, the Taliban rejected his proposal. Zabiullah Mujahid, a Taliban spokesman, put it very clearly: "The Taliban were united under the leadership of Mullah Muhammad Omar. All the fighters follow and obey orders of one central command. The existence of moderates and extremist elements within the rank and file of Taliban is wishful thinking of the West and the Afghan government."

Is it possible, as some have said, that the Taliban have mellowed since being toppled in 2001? This seems dubious. Muhammad Ibrahim Hanafi, a top Taliban commander, answered that question in an interview in March with CNN: "Our law is still the same old law which was in place during our rule in Afghanistan."

The only "reconciliation" strategy that is going to work is one between the Kabul government and the Afghan people. This requires a better communications strategy from the government, including having the president make addresses on TV and the radio and perhaps using cell phone technology to disseminate messages too. But the real key is making changes at the community level. Many local mullahs and citizens who have tolerated the Taliban in the past are open to working with a government that can protect them and help them find livelihoods. The government and its allies can best weaken the insurgency by better protecting the population, organizing local citizens' groups to cooperate on economic development, and hiring more people from every part of the country into the growing Afghan Army and police force.

How does working with tribal militias fit into this picture? It is appealing to ask local groups to help ensure security in their own communities and pay them in some way for that service. This can compensate for the slow growth in Afghan security forces to an extent; it also amounts to a reconciliation strategy, because it can include fighters who previously attacked government or NATO forces. Yet Afghans are understandably wary of anything that would re-arm the very groups that often contributed to civil war in the past, whether they go by tribal names or call themselves "private security companies." As such, NATO has pursued initiatives with tribes very carefully. But an approach tailored to Afghanistan's specific circumstances, known as the Community Defense Initiative, is now emerging. The Afghan government and NATO want to do any agreement on a community-wide basis (not a tribal basis), expecting elders to form a shura reflective of the various groups in a given region to oversee the effort. Armed groups would then be under government supervision and trained by NATO forces. The plan would avoid paying the fighters directly, instead providing funds to their communities for development projects. They would be expected not to allow the Taliban into their vicinities as a condition of any agreement. And of course they would not be allowed to do anything outside their own communities with their weapons; their jobs will be just to patrol where they live. To work, this approach requires the presence of NATO (or dependable Afghan) forces to provide supervision and if necessary enforcement— meaning that it is best viewed as a complement to McChrystal's troop buildup plan rather than an alternative.

The subject of reconciliation is a good way to conclude this discussion of current strategy because it underscores what our mission must achieve. In fact, this is a war, and certain core elements of the enemy simply must be defeated or marginalized. But by the same token, we must create the conditions of population security and law and order that make it hard for the insurgents to tap into local anger and find more recruits and more sympathizers for their cause. We cannot and should not reconcile with the true extremists; we must however reconcile with the mainstream of the Afghan population.

CHAPTER FOUR

Responding to the Critics

The Afghanistan war has understandably become controversial, given its long duration and lack of progress. Only one other war in American history rivals this one for its length, and that is Vietnam, so the parallels are unavoidable at one level. Critics have many fair concerns and all deserve response. In fact, after all the mistakes that have been made to date, after all the years and lives and dollars that have been squandered, the Afghanistan war may turn out to be unwinnable. But it is too soon to be fatalistic. More to the point, however, we believe that the war is not only winnable, but quite likely to be won—or at least contained and gradually quelled—provided that further, practical, achievable improvements in strategy are made over the next few months by both President Hamid Karzai and the international community. Most common criticisms of the current counterinsurgency effort can be rebutted directly and strongly. This chapter attempts that task.

CRITICISM 1: *"Afghans Always Hate, and Defeat, Invaders"*

This allegation is based largely on Afghanistan's long history of being at the crossroads of human movement and conflict and, more specifically, on its ability to defeat British forces in the nineteenth century and Soviet forces in the 1980s. To be sure, Afghans are worthy warriors; many Americans who have dealt with Iraqis and Afghans in recent years consider the latter to be better natural fighters.

But today's international presence in Afghanistan does not amount to an invasion. In contrast to the invaders of the past, today's international effort seeks only to help get Afghans on their feet well enough so that NATO can responsibly leave. The difference between U.S.-NATO goals, and the size and strength of our international coalition, and those of past invaders is stark. This is not meant as a naïve-sounding expression of the goodness of American motives. It is, rather, a fact, documented among other things by the reality that some forty countries are part of the International Security Assistance Force in Afghanistan today.[1]

Of course, not everyone believes what we say about our motives. Some think we intend to stay a long time; others believe we are not really trying hard to succeed. To the extent that we fail in the effort, our motives will surely continue to be doubted, and support for our presence will continue to weaken, as has been the case in recent times. But just as in Iraq, if we can successfully convey the sense that we are building up capability now so we can more rapidly and successfully build it *down* later, we have a chance to gain adequate Afghan support.[2] Indeed, for all the reduction in our popularity this decade, the international community is still far more popular in Afghanistan than it was in Iraq when the surge began—and certainly more popular than the Soviets or other previous invaders ever were.

In the 1980s, the United States, Saudi Arabia, and others helped the Afghan resistance movement that eventually forced the Soviets to withdraw, so there is some common history of cooperation predating the current war effort. Moreover, the Afghan resistance to the Soviet invasion and its own communist government was a broad-based movement, whereas today's Taliban-led insurgency draws support primarily from the Ghilzai tribal confederation, and some other lesser groups, within the Pashtun community. As well, the anti-Soviet resistance may have included up to a quarter million fighters; the Taliban and other insurgents in Afghanistan today may number 25,000 or so.[3]

The Taliban and other militias do benefit from some help from abroad today, particularly from elements within Pakistan. But it is on a smaller scale than the help the mujahedin received in the 1980s. Improved border security as well as support for stronger steps by Pakistan against extremists on its territory could further reduce this assistance.

CRITICISM 2: *"Foreign Troops Only Make the Problem Worse"*

This related charge, voiced in 2008 by none other than the British ambassador to Afghanistan himself, Sir Sherard Cowper-Coles, suggests that Afghans will do better if we leave them to their own devices—perhaps supplying some aid but otherwise strictly limiting our involvement. Cowper-Coles is highly regarded, and his observation must be taken seriously.[4]

The basis for his argument is that Afghans dislike foreigners enough that our very presence in Afghanistan weakens the Karzai government by association. Because NATO is fighting to help his government, so goes the reasoning, its unpopularity spills over onto him. NATO's reassuring presence may also discourage him from taking tough steps—firing corrupt officials, for example—needed to build a stable country.

To be sure, popular anger at NATO has increased greatly over the years; eventually, we may reach a point of no return and no longer be able to win back the support of the Afghan people. But in fact, Afghans do not hate foreigners categorically. NATO was very popular in the war's early going, when it was seen as the agent that had driven the Taliban from power. Yes, we have squandered much of that good will, but by virtue of doing our job badly, not by virtue of our very presence.

For all the unpopularity of the United States in Afghanistan, our popularity there is still better than it was in Iraq before the surge, as noted—and far better than it was among Iraqi Sunnis. Indeed, while only 32 percent of Afghans had a favorable opinion of NATO in early 2009, meaning that over 60 percent had a negative opinion, in Iraq only about 20 percent wanted coalition forces to remain in early 2007, and 61 percent of the population (and more than 90 percent of all Sunnis) thought it acceptable to *attack* NATO forces.[5] Yet Iraqi Sunnis—those most resistant to the coalition presence—nonetheless came to be our allies and partners in the past three years, as the Anbar Awakening aligned our interests, and more successful American tactics limited the degree of Sunni hatred of the United States. This recent lesson suggests that it is often possible to rebuild even a severely strained relationship in a wartime setting—especially if the other party really needs the help.

Moreover, July 2009 polls in Afghanistan indicated that U.S. and NATO popularity had returned, at least temporarily, to the 60 percent range, as had Afghans' optimism about the future and their favorability scores for their own president and army (actually the army scored even higher, in the 80 percent range). These numbers have probably sagged since then, because of the disputed presidential race among other problems, but they do suggest that Afghans are not fundamentally opposed to the international community's efforts to help them. Nor are they fundamentally pessimistic about the future; in fact, quite the contrary.[6]

When considering the idea that we simply must leave now, it is important to remember the real options. Afghan security forces are not up to the challenge of protecting their own country now; they are too small, too badly trained, and still too infested with incompetents as well as individuals playing both sides.

Looking over the whole eight-year experience in Afghanistan to date, it would seem that the approach of minimizing the role of foreign forces has already been tried and found wanting. In the early years, foreign troops were based only in Kabul, then only in Kabul and the immediate vicinity—and the overall situation deteriorated.

Admittedly, time is not on our side right now, and the population is losing a good deal of its earlier hopefulness. If we continue to fail in Afghanistan much longer, we may in fact lose our ability to find Afghans willing to work with us, and may strengthen any and all forces opposing us. But the Afghan government and NATO remain much more popular than the Taliban, even in Pashtun regions, suggesting that we have one last chance to get this right. At the same time, we must avoid assuming that, just because they are unpopular, the Taliban can never retake power. In fact, the Taliban were never popular but dominated by using violence and fear to make people compliant. If they retake large swaths of land and appear to have the momentum, fear and compliance may again take hold in the population. So we must break that dynamic, and as soon as possible.

CRITICISM 3: *"Afghanistan Is Much Harder than Iraq"*

Ironically, this argument is probably offered more by supporters of the current mission than by its opponents. Their intentions are understandable. Often it is U.S. officials, like Defense Secretary Gates, who make this point, seemingly to brace the American people for a tough road ahead.[7]

To be sure, there are ways in which Afghanistan is more complicated than Iraq. And in some specific ways, admittedly, it may be harder. The number of tribes is larger, the drug problem is worse, and the country is not blessed with the oil resources that Iraq has. The sanctuary for insurgent fighters available in Pakistan is even harder to control than, say, the Iraq-Syria border. The dearth of Afghan professionals after three decades of war—and an increasingly successful Taliban campaign of assassination and intimidation in recent years as well—poses a serious challenge to stable management of the government.

But that same history of war makes the Afghan people realistic in their expectations about the future and grateful for even modest progress, as polls show. Afghans were overwhelmingly supportive of us in the early years and, as noted, remain far less hostile to foreigners even today than were Iraqis during most of the war there. The sanctuary in Pakistan is a very serious problem, but the flow of foreign fighters into Iraq (largely through Syria) and the flow of advanced weapons into Iraq from Iran were huge problems too. Drug production, trafficking, and use are a big problem in Afghanistan, but corruption, including corruption within the oil trade, has been extremely problematic in Iraq. While Afghanistan's relative lack of easily exploitable natural resources constitutes a challenge for the country, in the short term foreign resources can largely compensate, given the current commitment of the international community to this important mission. (Over time, of course, these natural resources will have to be better developed.)

The levels of violence in Iraq in the middle of this decade, before the surge, were far worse than anything Afghanistan has experienced since 2001. For a three- to four-year period, about ten times as many Iraqi civilians were killed every year as were killed in Afghanistan in 2009. Only in the past two years have the rates of civilian casualties in Iraq dropped to anything close to those in Afghanistan. Tens of thousands of Iraqi professionals were driven out of the country or killed; whole communities were disrupted and displaced; and sectarian tensions were inflamed far more broadly in Iraq than they have been in Afghanistan. To be sure, Afghanistan is hard enough. But on balance, making major progress there should be as doable as it was in Iraq.

All that said, we finish with a note of caution: in Iraq before the surge, the United States was extremely wary of the government of Prime Minister Nouri al-Maliki. Even during the first months of the surge, the type of top-down political compromise that was viewed as crucial did not occur very quickly. But then Maliki and other Iraqi leaders improved their performance—reaching some deals on matters like the annual budget and de-Baathification reform, challenging and when necessary attacking Shiite militias from Basra to Sadr City, and reforming institutions like the national police. In Afghanistan, despite a few hopeful signs here and there, the government has not yet proven itself a viable partner in fighting extremism and corruption. Until it does, the idea that the Afghanistan mission is just as "winnable" as Iraq will remain a theory, not a provable proposition.

CRITICISM 4: *"Afghanistan Is Less Important than Iraq"*

On the campaign trail, Barack Obama criticized President Bush for being distracted by Iraq at the expense of the mission in Afghanistan, which Obama considered more important. But it is also possible to argue the opposite—that given where we are today, regardless of whether or not we should have fought the Iraq war, it is more important to consolidate gains in Iraq than to rush to reinforce our troop presence in Afghanistan. At the moment this is not a pressing issue, because the buildup in Afghanistan does not require an accelerated drawdown in Iraq. By the end of 2010 we are to have 150,000 U.S. troops in the two countries combined, less than at any point since 2003. The pace of the withdrawal from Iraq has been determined by Washington and Baghdad and reflects security conditions within Iraq as well as the growing military capabilities and political confidence of the Iraqi government. But this situation could change if the Iraq mission becomes more nettlesome in the coming months. So are we setting ourselves up for trouble in Iraq with our new emphasis on Afghanistan?

The basis for the claim that Iraq matters more than Afghanistan is that Iraq is a major oil-producing country in the heart of the strategically crucial Middle East. It is also a country that, in the past, has built and used weapons of mass destruction; invaded neighbors, destabilizing the region; and supported terrorism against Israel. Afghanistan by contrast is remote, and with relatively few natural resources and relatively little inherent economic or strategic importance. The argument that Iraq is more important thus has some merit.

However, Afghanistan has greater importance than this argument allows, for at least three reasons. First and most simply, it has been and could easily again become a major refuge for senior al Qaeda leaders, who still have major designs against the West and can be quite innovative and lethal when they are able to sustain a viable command structure.[8] This was revealed, for example, in the organization's sophisticated plot in 2006—thwarted by British intelligence—to blow up a number of airplanes over the Atlantic simultaneously. Al Qaeda also still has ambitions to carry out even deadlier attacks, perhaps even using weapons of mass destruction.[9] Most senior al Qaeda figures are probably now on the Pakistan side of the border, but that is only because it is temporarily safer, a situation that could change if Afghanistan were abandoned by the West. Better to squeeze from both sides of the border, working with our allies to do so, than to allow a sanctuary on either side.

Second, Afghanistan has become a symbol and a focal point of the broader war on terror. How the United States and its allies deal with Afghanistan will be widely studied by those evaluating the West's resolve against al Qaeda and related movements. It will also be scrutinized by those who wonder if the West really cares about the well-being of Muslim allies and really feels any moral commitment to their security and to their prospects for democracy and for economic growth, unless they happen to have oil. By this perspective, Afghanistan has already been betrayed by the West. We largely abandoned the country after the Soviets pulled out in 1989 even as it fell into a Hobbesian anarchy with competing warlords, featuring extensive shelling of the capital city of Kabul among other horrors, followed by the Taliban takeover of the country. To give up on the country again would be a clear signal that the United States was fundamentally undependable. It would also provide al Qaeda and its allies with fodder for their arguments that their global struggle against Western "infidels" was clearly succeeding—a message that might help them in future recruiting.

Third, instability in Afghanistan probably creates more instability in nuclear-armed Pakistan. Admittedly, this is not immediately obvious. In recent years, however, our efforts to defeat the Taliban in Afghanistan may have indirectly *worsened* the situation in Pakistan. We drove some of the Afghan Taliban into Pakistan, where they were tolerated by many Pakistani military and intelligence personnel who viewed them as a hedge in case the Western world gave up on the Afghanistan mission. Once inside Pakistan, in places like Quetta, the Afghan Taliban then intermingled with and strengthened Pakistani Taliban, who subsequently attacked their own countrymen in places like the Swat Valley. Arguably, doing the Afghan job badly has therefore made the Pakistan situation worse, at least at the margins. In addition, U.S. air strikes against Afghan insurgents taking refuge inside Pakistan worsen America's image in Pakistan and complicate U.S. abilities to work in some ways with Pakistanis against their domestic threats.[10]

But this argument should not be overdone; the Taliban movement within Pakistan is mostly indigenous to Pakistan. Even more to the point, if NATO and friendly Afghan forces lost the war in Afghanistan, Taliban fighters of all persuasions would be provided a sanctuary from which to carry out further destabilizing attacks against Pakistan and the rest of the world. Especially now that the Pakistani military shows signs of getting tougher on its own insurgents, allowing the Pakistani Taliban such an escape valve within Afghanistan would be dangerous to Pakistan's own future and further threaten that nuclear-armed state. At this point at least, instability in Afghanistan would probably bleed over into Pakistan and make the latter's problems even worse.

Sometimes advocates of downsizing in Afghanistan imply that we could conduct counterterrorism raids against any future threats there from long distance. This is quite unlikely. Unlike the case with, say, Yemen or Somalia, there is no available coastline or international airspace to use in approaching Afghanistan. We would need a partner willing to let us operate from its territory, which might or might not be attainable. It is hard to see why a future Afghan government would want to allow us small bases for counterterrorism missions on its soil, if we had otherwise abandoned the country, especially since that government would probably be Taliban-run.

We have the force levels required to prosecute efforts in both Iraq and Afghanistan at once, albeit at great sacrifice by our men and women in uniform. And it makes sense to try to do both.

CRITICISM 5: *"We Should Just Do Counterterrorism, not Counterinsurgency, in Afghanistan"*

This common argument literally accepts what President Obama said in releasing his strategy in March—that our goal in Afghanistan should be limited to going after those who attacked us on 9/11.

The problem with just doing counterterrorism—in addition to the fact that we largely already tried it during the Bush administration with little success—is that it misunderstands how counterterrorism is conducted. The key to successful counterterrorism is good intelligence. Because top al Qaeda leaders have learned not to use cell phones, satellite phones, or other devices whose signals might be intercepted by American intelligence, and because its military assets and operational centers are not large enough to be spotted from afar by aircraft or spy satellites, we need to get our information on the ground. That does not necessarily require American soldiers, but it does require developing trust and relationships with local populations. These populations in turn will not give information to foreign forces that are present one day, gone the next—leaving the informers to face revenge attacks from the insurgents and extremists.

Narrow counterterrorism tactics of a surgical nature have been tried in Afghanistan (and in Iraq, for four years before the surge). They have generally failed, as evidenced most strikingly by the Taliban's comeback. They will almost surely fail again if that is all we do. Moreover, even if we were lucky enough to pick off Osama bin Laden or Ayman al-Zawahiri, we would not at this point be lucky enough to check the movements that have so destabilized both Afghanistan and Pakistan in recent years. The Taliban and al Qaeda and other extremists have by now become interwoven with each other, making it hard if not impossible to identify a core enemy. A more comprehensive strategy—something along the lines of clear, hold, build—is the only promising approach. Admittedly, this strategy is itself very hard: in 2009 even in places where NATO, with Afghan help, can clear, there exist neither adequate Afghan forces to hold nor sufficient Afghan and international governance and development capacity to build. These gaps in our strategy must be redressed. Thankfully, President Obama's December 1 policy change is doing so.

CRITICISM 6: *"The U.S. Military Is for War Fighting, Not Nation Building"*

In fact, this mantra was a fairly common philosophy for the incoming Bush administration back in 2001—until the tide of history made George W. Bush the president most preoccupied with nation building since Harry Truman.

The debate about whether the United States armed forces should do nation building was a big deal in the 1990s. But now it is over, and the nation builders have won the debate hands down. The terminology has shifted, to be sure, from nation building to "stabilization and reconstruction" missions. And few people of any political stripe or ideological bent find these missions enjoyable, so in that sense those averse to this type of mission are in good company. But there is no longer any real disagreement about whether the military should do these kinds of things.

In fact, the Department of Defense recognized as much four years into the Afghanistan operation and two and a half years into the Iraq war, while Donald Rumsfeld was still secretary of defense. In a November 2005 directive, he stated:

> Stability operations are a core U.S. military mission that the Department of Defense shall be prepared to conduct and support. They shall be given priority comparable to combat operations and be explicitly addressed and integrated across all DoD activities including doctrine, organizations, training, education, exercises, materiel, leadership, personnel, facilities, and planning.[11]

A major Army manual released in October 2008 repeated the same message, underscoring that stability operations were as important to U.S. ground forces as both classic offense and classic defense and were perhaps more likely to determine the outcome of a complex military mission than either of these other types of operations.[12] The National Intelligence Council concurs that irregular warfare will only increase in frequency in the future, making such U.S. operations continuously relevant.[13]

In fairness to the critics of nation building, they usefully helped shift the rhetoric away from nation building and toward stabilization and reconstruction—or "state building," perhaps. The nation-building language implies greater power for foreigners than they really have (or want); only Afghans can ultimately build an Afghan nation, and our role is to help provide security, training, and economic development while they create their own tools to do so. As such, the NATO mission should be viewed as helping to empower and enable Afghans, not as doing their job for them.

CRITICISM 7: *"We Should Negotiate with the Taliban"*

To be sure, we should negotiate with local affiliates of the Taliban. And as time goes on, if we gain battlefield momentum, we may even be able to persuade some of the Taliban leadership to negotiate—largely on our terms. But the notion of a compromise today with the central Taliban leadership is flawed for two reasons.

First, wars do not usually end through negotiation. They end when someone wins.[14] Second, as argued earlier, the Taliban as such are not interested in negotiation and are not the sort of organization with whom we should want to negotiate—meaning compromise. Their extremist ideology is misogynous, intolerant, and ruthless. Their history in Afghanistan has been brutal and barbaric. They are extremely unpopular among Afghans, particularly in non-Pashtun areas, where their public support is virtually nil, but even in places like Kandahar, where despite recent strides, the Taliban garner only a 25 percent favorability rating (compared with a 75 percent rating for the government, despite years of failed efforts there). The Taliban are on a roll, but their success is based more on a combination of intimidation and a general perception among Afghans that they are winning ("Nothing succeeds like success," as the saying goes, and Afghans know how to pick the winning side). That momentum is not based on a fundamental appeal to most Afghans, however, and we should be able to reverse it with a more successful strategy.

Negotiation still has a very important role, as many have argued.[15] Most Afghan insurgents, perhaps 75 percent according to estimates of David Kilcullen, are in fact *not* hard-core Taliban—and it is best not to call them moderate Taliban either. They are, rather, local disaffected citizens and tribal leaders, upset by the government's fecklessness, perhaps impressed by recent Taliban gains, and often feeling aggrieved about life. In short, to use Kilcullen's ingenious phrase, they are "accidental guerrillas." They can probably be won over by a combination of greater security, various types of incentives to participate in government, a healthier basis for rural economic activity focused on production of legal crops, and other such signs of progress that the new strategy should make possible. Admittedly, some aspects of this effort will be harder than others, especially given the high levels of corruption in the current Afghan government. But most elements of this strategy are within our ability to pursue.

More NATO success in killing and capturing Taliban and other insurgents could help, too, by reversing perceptions among Afghan citizens about who is winning the war. However, NATO and Afghan forces need to be careful not to kill those guerrillas who may actually be seeking to negotiate; too often in the past, "blacklisting" of individuals has led to the killing or capture and long detention of resistance fighters who might in fact have wanted to talk with us. This is another very important and delicate aspect of our strategy that poor intelligence about the Afghan tribal structure, combined with a decimation of much of that structure over the past thirty years of war, complicates enormously. But U.S. and NATO forces are, belatedly, conducting "human terrain mapping" of the country in an effort to identify viable partners for negotiation and cooperation in the future. These efforts are crucial. They are overdue, but they are now being made.

Capturing extremists may generally be better than killing them, where possible, because it allows us to use improved prison rehabilitation programs to try to moderate some. Such programs should not generally consist of lectures by Westerners but should be led by Afghan mullahs and other authorities who can show prisoners that Islam does not countenance the killing of innocents. We can simultaneously provide job training, as was done in Iraq rather successfully, in these prisons.[16]

CRITICISM 8: *"U.S. Allies Aren't Really Committed to the Fight"*

This criticism takes note of the fact that many European allies in Afghanistan have sought to reduce the risk of casualties to their forces by placing severe restrictions on what they are allowed to do. The effect of this policy is to constrain the options for the NATO commander when he needs to reinforce troops in a dangerous, troubled part of the country. Another concern is that, even after the election of Barack Obama, with his promises of a more multilateral and cooperative style of American leadership, foreign countries have been prepared to offer only a very modest number of added forces (or other resources, for that matter) to the effort.

However, it is important to remember what the allies have done. NATO invoked the Article V mutual defense clause of its treaty after September 11, and most NATO countries have contributed to the Afghanistan war effort even though Afghanistan is thousands of miles away from Europe (where the self-defense pact was originally designed to apply). Even countries with powerful historical and political constraints on their actions, like Germany, have deployed troops, often in considerable numbers.

Half a dozen countries—including Britain, Canada, Denmark, the Netherlands, France, and Australia—have done a great deal in this war and taken substantial risks with their troops. Canada, for example, has basically revamped its entire military, not to mention its national strategic culture, after decades in which its soldiers never saw combat and in which its citizens and politicians became very averse to the risk of casualties. Now, Canada has suffered higher losses per capita than has the United States, measured either against the size of its overall population or against the number of troops it has deployed to the mission.

In the summer of 2009, America's allies collectively reached a distressing milestone—their 500th fatality in Afghanistan (those numbers have since increased; meanwhile, as of early 2010 U.S. fatalities are tragically closing in on the 1,000 milestone). As of June, the United Kingdom had suffered 165, Canada 118, Germany 30 (despite the caveats), France 28, Spain 25, Denmark 21, the Netherlands 19, Italy 14, Romania 11, Australia 10, Poland 9, and Norway 4. Korea, the Czech Republic, Hungary, Portugal, Sweden, Finland, and each of the three Baltic states had lost either one, two, or three soldiers. Since then operations have resulted in even more casualties, especially to the British. This is a far cry from a feckless alliance.

The caveats on some countries' troops are a problem, to be sure. It would be nice if Germany, Spain, Italy and the Scandinavian countries, among others, made their forces readily available for missions nationwide—day and night, big and small, safe and unsafe. In fact, many soldiers from these countries have said they wish that their countries' political processes would allow them to play a larger role in the actual war.

But we should not make the best the enemy of the good. Suggestions that all caveats be removed are unrealistic and indeed counterproductive.[17] Moreover, in those parts of Afghanistan where casualty-averse allies are operating, conditions are often less dangerous, and the caveats on the soldiers therefore less locally debilitating. Northern and western Afghanistan do resemble countries with peacekeeping missions more than war-fighting ones, in contrast to the east and south. Yes, there are problems of burden sharing associated with a war in which Americans, British, Canadians, and a few others are doing most of the dying on behalf of the foreign coalition. But while this situation raises serious issues of fairness, it does not necessarily cause basic doubt about the viability of the mission. And yes, some allies are tiring of this war even faster than is the American public. The Dutch are due to end their involvement in 2010, the Canadians in 2011. But their frustration is understandable, given trends of recent years. These planned departures should be seen as a challenge to policymakers to quickly fix the problems that have festered in our strategy in Afghanistan for so long. It may be too late to reverse the attitudes of each and every ally looking to leave, but it should not be too late to maintain an impressive coalition providing real combat help to the United States and the Afghan government.

CRITICISM 9: *"There Is No Exit Strategy or Exit Schedule"*

It is true that we cannot know when the United States and its allies would leave Afghanistan. But we can sketch out a rough sense of the schedule, even now. The war should not be open-ended.

There are several reasons to believe that if the new strategy is successful, we will see clear evidence of that by late 2010 or 2011. We should then be able to contemplate major reductions in the size of the U.S. military presence in Afghanistan by roughly 2012 or 2013. This timing would be consistent with the pledge of President Karzai in his November 19, 2009, inaugural address as he began his second term, when he predicted that the Afghan army could begin to assume control of many operations by 2012. Of course an ongoing effort will be needed for a few years thereafter, but at gradually diminishing troop levels.

We explain the reasons for this rough schedule in chapter five. Here, we offer just one suggestive argument, based on an analogy with Iraq. There, the surge showed clear signs of success by late summer of 2007, about seven to eight months after the new strategy had been announced in January 2007 and shortly after the U.S. troop buildup was concluded in June.

But in Afghanistan, everything tends to move only about half as fast as in Iraq. The 2009 troop buildup took more than six months, and the 2010 buildup will likely require as long. Still, by the end of 2010, the NATO troop configuration should be roughly complete, and by early 2011 Afghan security forces should exceed a quarter million in strength, more than halfway toward the ultimate goal—with most having benefited from some months of partnering and apprenticeship by then.

It should be kept in mind that Afghanistan's levels of violence, while serious, have been far less than those in Iraq at any time from 2004 to 2007. That makes it harder to see immediate improvements in the statistics once a new strategy is implemented. But with 400,000 competent coalition forces on the ground by early 2011, perhaps twice the late 2009 total, we should see substantial progress.

CRITICISM 10: *"We Can't Really Bring Afghanistan into the Twenty-First Century"*

This critique alleges that Afghanistan is such a conservative, rural, tribal, and traditional land that any Western-led effort at democratization and modernization of the country is bound to fail. Some suggest that our efforts to promote the equality of women, integrate the country with the outside world, and strengthen the urban-based government of the country will simply inflame the anger and opposition of many Afghans, especially Pashtuns living in villages and towns in the south of the country, where the extremist message of the Taliban has the most resonance.

This argument is wrong for two principal reasons. First, most Afghans do want to live in the twenty-first century. Their enthusiasm for the 2009 presidential election campaign—if not necessarily for its tainted outcome—demonstrated their interest in democratic elections, for example.[18] Second, NATO will not force more change on them than they are ready to accept themselves.

To be sure, elements of Afghanistan are quite conservative, and issues such as religious tolerance and gender equality will take time to address. But that is in part what the normal peacetime development process in coming decades is for. The imperative now is to win the war and defeat the insurgency. Some reforms can be undertaken now, to the extent that Afghans themselves want them. In fact, they already are happening; some two million Afghan girls are in school, for example. Other changes can happen gradually.

As for what Afghans want, just look at the polls. People consistently oppose the Taliban. This survey result cannot come from fear of the Taliban—if individuals were giving the answers they thought Taliban elements wanted them to give, they would be pro-Taliban rather than anti-Taliban. And while many Afghans indicate dissatisfaction with the Afghan government and with the foreign presence, that dissatisfaction has so far not turned into any meaningful support for the Taliban. The surveys seem reasonably accurate, consistent from one to another, and reflective of a people's desire for a more modern and democratic life.

As for what NATO is after, it is trying primarily to provide security for the population, build up Afghan security forces, create roads and better utilities, improve health care and education, and provide the people with economic alternatives to opium. It is hard to fault these goals or to believe they run counter to Afghan culture or mores. For the most part, Afghans have expressed anger with NATO because of its failure to deliver on such goals—not because of the goals themselves. And while the country may not reach desired levels of education, health care, and other quality-of-life indicators soon, simply getting on the right path will win over most Afghans—as was evident a few years back, when economic conditions were worse than they are now, but public opinion was much more favorable toward NATO because trends were generally in the right direction.

CRITICISM 11: *"We Are Refighting Vietnam"*

The Afghan war is surpassing Vietnam as the country's longest war, so it is natural to draw the analogy. And, to be fair, there are echoes of Vietnam in Afghanistan, besides the obvious one of a long war—the gradual escalation of U.S. force totals with time under multiple presidents, the remoteness of the country and the culture from most Americans' experience, the vagueness with which the stakes are defined (given that neither Vietnam nor Afghanistan is at the center of world industry or commerce), and the high stakes attributed to both conflicts that make it very hard for supporters to imagine the possibility of defeat.

But in most other ways, the wars could not be more different. Vietnam was part of a broader cold war struggle and was seen as a pawn or domino in that contest. Afghanistan is seen as linked to Pakistan, but not to many other countries, and important on its own terms given the presence of al Qaeda and other extremists in its part of the world. The Vietnam war typically caused more than 5,000 U.S. deaths a year, and over 100,000 Vietnamese deaths annually; the Afghan war, as terrible as it is, is far less deadly. In fact, NATO losses are measured in the hundreds per year; Afghan civilian fatalities are in the low thousands, and most of the latter are due to insurgent action.

This is more than a statistical anomaly or a random factoid. It is crucial to understanding the war. Our struggle in Afghanistan has been handled, with all due respect to those brave Americans who served their country in Vietnam, with far more precision and discretion in the use of force. And as troubled as Afghanistan has been this decade, it is probably a better place to live than it was before—in contrast to what happened in Vietnam, where the war made things much worse than they had been (even if the war was not truly caused by the United States there either).

There have been episodes of good American performance at counterinsurgency in the past. But they have been interludes, exceptions to the rule. The Marines did a good job with their Combined Action Program during part of the Vietnam war, for example. The U.S. armed forces performed reasonably well in the Philippines just over a century ago too. But these were clearly exceptions, not the rule. Most of the U.S. military overapplied firepower in Vietnam, for example.

After Vietnam, the U.S. military reverted to training and equipping its units for traditional high-intensity maneuver operations rather than more complex missions. Occasional efforts to study "low-intensity operations" that characterize counterinsurgency actions were focused on very specific parts of the armed forces, and greater efforts in the 1990s to prepare for peace operations were seen largely as distractions from true military missions. Only in the last three years has the core of the U.S. armed forces treated counterinsurgency missions as truly important. That too is a departure from Vietnam and, for that matter, from most other periods in American history.[19]

Today, both our theory and our practice of counterinsurgency are sound. Commanders as well as troops have thought hard about how to fight these kinds of wars and put many principles into action. Consider some of the powerful, persuasive adages and rules of thumb that appear in the military's 2006 field manual and that are taught to troops and their commanders; these come from the section on "paradoxes" in counterinsurgency and reflect how nuanced American military understanding of such missions has become:[20]

—Sometimes, the more you protect your force, the less secure you may be

—Sometimes, the more force is used, the less effective it is

—Sometimes doing nothing is the best reaction

—Some of the best weapons for counterinsurgents do not shoot

—The host nation doing something tolerably is normally better than us doing it well

—Tactical success guarantees nothing

—Many important decisions are not made by generals

Summing up the above arguments, we can simply say that most Afghans want the current mission to succeed, NATO troops know how to carry it out, many Afghans in and out of uniform are proving committed to the effort, and the resources for the effort are increasingly commensurate with the magnitude of the challenge. We have a very good chance of succeeding, keeping in mind that our goals need to be realistic and focused on protecting the population while building up Afghan security forces and governance capacities more generally.

But in light of the difficulty of this mission, we will finish this chapter with a recognition that not all criticisms and worries can be rebutted. First, while the Afghanistan war is far less deadly, is doing far more to improve the well-being of the indigenous population, and is being fought far more carefully and prudently than was the Vietnam War, there is one disturbing parallel. To date, the Afghan government is not up to the job of being a viable partner in this mission for NATO forces and the international community; despite having some good people, it is still too plagued by corruption, nepotism, and sheer incompetence. A counter-insurgency campaign cannot be won without a solid domestic partner to any international presence; as was true in Vietnam for so long, we currently lack such a viable host government in Afghanistan. In coming months the Karzai government must show improvement by changing the climate of impunity for corrupt officials and warlords. The worst of the worst must go, and tribes and communities that feel disadvantaged by the system of governance (and spoils) must be enfranchised.

Second, it must be acknowledged that into 2009 the Taliban had the momentum in this war. Violence is worse in Afghanistan now than at any time since 2001. The Taliban are active in more than one-third of the country's nearly 400 districts, after having negligible presence in the country half a decade ago. Their campaigns of terror and intimida-tion are weakening the government as well as popular support for the government in places like Kandahar (to say nothing of popular support in the United States and other NATO countries). Another year or two of trends like this and the war could be lost. The fact that most people in Afghanistan lead better lives than they did under Taliban rule in the 1990s, with greater access to schools and health care, and higher average incomes, is true but insufficient. Negative security trends are beginning to trump progress in quality of life.

So there is a lot of work to do, and to do soon. How will we know if we are beginning to make headway? And how can our strategy be further modified so that our prospects for at least moderate success improve? These are the questions addressed in the book's last two chapters.

CHAPTER FIVE

Measuring Progress— and Figuring Out an Exit Plan

"Going forward [in Afghanistan], we will not blindly stay the course. Instead, we will set clear metrics to measure progress and hold ourselves accountable."
—President Barack Obama, March 27, 2009

How can we tell if a counterinsurgency campaign is being won? In the course of 2010 and 2011 it will be very important to know how to answer this question in Afghanistan. Even if the current U.S. NATO-led strategy is increasingly robust and correct, and even if it is improved further in ways we suggest in the next chapter, it is important to recognize that the effort could still fail. The situation could simply be hopeless at this late hour, after so many years of floundering that have cost NATO and President Hamid Karzai so much credibility and allowed the Taliban to regroup. Even if the situation still offers hope, and even if NATO does its part, the Karzai government may fail to play its own role. No counterinsurgency campaign can succeed without the considerable efforts of the indigenous government, which in the end is the only organization that can be legitimate in the eyes of its citizens and provide a true rallying point for those who wish to build up their country and defeat their insurgency. The international community may also continue to reinforce certain unhealthy tendencies of the Karzai government itself—providing too many contracts to corrupt individuals, allowing subcontracting procedures that have the result of creating multiple opportunities for bribes and commissions, paying individuals like Ahmed Wali Karzai for their supposed help in certain places despite the culture of corruption and impunity that such individuals perpetuate.

The template of counterinsurgency that was effective in Iraq may not be transplantable to Afghanistan. At a basic conceptual level, it could prove to be the wrong strategy for Afghanistan. Or, perhaps more likely, even if the same basic principles are largely applicable in both places, we may simply fail at a practical level to find the necessary national, provincial, and local leaders with whom to cooperate. Despite all the improvements made by President Obama and others in recent months, we could still suffer defeat. We need a way to know if we are succeeding in this core goal.

Assessing progress in counterinsurgency missions is always hard. Sizing the force correctly for a stabilization mission is a key ingredient—and it has been the subject of much discussion in the modern American debate. But in fact, there is no exact formula for sizing forces. Even if there were, getting the numbers right would hardly ensure success. Troops might not perform optimally if they are poorly prepared for the mission; the security environment might pose too many daunting challenges for even properly sized and trained forces to contend with; the politics of the country in question might not support the efforts of the troops because of the actions of internal or external spoilers.

Only by tracking progress on the ground can we know whether a strategy is working. And only by examining a range of indicators can we determine how to adjust a strategy that may require improvement. The process of defeating an insurgency while building up a host government is too complex to lend itself to simple quantification; assessing trends in such a mission is equal parts art and science, so there is no short list of metrics to provide a definitive bottom line on how things are going, Indeed, those who try to use a short list often cherry-pick data to serve an agenda. As Fred Ikle, former under secretary of defense from the Reagan years, once said about an analogous situation, "Both sides in the internal debate often pick some isolated statistics out of the welter of information, instead of trying to justify their position on the basis on an overall evaluation."[1] We must beware of this temptation.

A number of axioms have been developed over the decades to guide policymakers as they attempt counterinsurgency, stabilization, and nation-building missions. Several concepts have become so frequently voiced that they have developed almost iconic status:

—Counterinsurgency requires attention to three main areas of effort: security, economics, and politics.

—Successful counterinsurgency depends most critically on how the local population views its well-being and the role of the government and international forces in supporting that well-being.

—Battlefield victories are important but do not ensure success.

—Successful counterinsurgency requires empowerment of legitimate, indigenous actors and cannot be achieved principally through the efforts of outsiders.

—Patience is required in counterinsurgency, because successful efforts typically take a decade or longer.

—Care and precision are required in the use of force in counterinsurgency; policing functions are ultimately more appropriate than combat operations by soldiers.

The problem with such a list of truisms is not so much that they are incorrect—in fact, they are probably all generally sound. Rather, the challenge comes in translating these principles into actionable policy in a given case and then determining if the translation is succeeding. It is here where metrics potentially have their greatest role.

Metrics are easy to misuse. In Vietnam, for example, the United States was convinced that there would be a "crossover point" in attrition of the Viet Cong. If U.S. military forces could manage to kill enough of them, say 50,000 a year, their recruiting efforts would not be able to keep pace, and combined American and South Vietnamese forces would ultimately prevail. This focus on body counts contributed to General William Westmoreland's unfortunate emphasis on search-and-destroy operations, which caused huge numbers of civilian casualties and in that way increased the enemy's capacity to recruit from an angry population. The United States and South Vietnam also fixated on the ratio of counterinsurgents to insurgents, working from the assumption that successful counterinsurgency requires ten government soldiers for every insurgent. This simplifying assumption is partly validated by history, but only in an approximate sense. By applying it too rigidly, the rule of thumb misled American and South Vietnamese policymakers, giving them too much confidence that they would be successful if they could just generate a certain number of combat forces (without paying sufficient attention to the forces' quality).[2]

This unhappy Vietnam experience with metrics is one reason why U.S. commanders have been reluctant to offer estimates of the size of the enemy in Iraq and Afghanistan. The noted Australian soldier and scholar David Kilcullen has estimated that the Taliban in 2008 numbered from 32,000 to 40,000 fighters inside Afghanistan at any moment, with about 8,000 to 10,000 of them making up the hard-core full-time movement. Major General Mart de Kruif, former commander of ISAF forces in southern Afghanistan, estimated that in his sector, notably Kandahar and Helmand provinces as well as Zabul and Uruzgan, the resistance numbered perhaps 10,000 to 18,000 fighters in the summer of 2009 "including the $10-a-day fighters."[3] General McChrystal estimated the size of the full-time insurgency at about 25,000 in his congressional testimony on December 9, 2009. By contrast, the mujahedin who fought the Soviets in the 1980s may have numbered up to 250,000, and they were supplied with advanced arms by Pakistan, the United States, and Saudi Arabia.[4] That said, if the Afghan resistance is continually increasing, it is difficult to take much solace in the fact that it is not huge. So trying to track its size is worthwhile, so long as numbers are recognized to be highly imprecise.

Iraq provides context too. Many lessons learned from Vietnam were put into practice there, but mistakes still occurred in the use of metrics. For example, we thought that Iraqi security forces were improving fast in the 2004–06 period as we recruited, trained, and equipped. But those forces were usually badly led, often by sectarian actors with ties to extremist militias, and in retrospect (as scholar Steven Biddle had earlier warned) our efforts had the partial effect of arming antagonists in a civil war. Most metrics failed to capture such trends—until we factored battlefield performance into official assessments.

That Iraq experience provides one valuable lesson for Afghanistan. Others come from earlier successful counterinsurgency and stabilization missions in places such as the Philippines and Malaya. Many of the metrics used there placed a premium on tracking trends in the daily life of typical citizens. How secure were they, and whom did they credit for that security? How hopeful did they find their economic situation, regardless of the nation's GDP or even their own personal wealth at a moment in time? Did they think their country's politics were giving them a voice?[5]

METRICS IN AFGHANISTAN

So understanding the pitfalls and limitations of metrics—but also realizing there is little choice but to try to assess progress in this type of war through some sort of structured analysis, rather than just the impressions of leaders—how can we tell if the Afghanistan war is headed in the right direction? Which metrics are most important, when should they reveal progress if indeed the current strategy winds up working—and, by contrast, how can we know if the strategy is not working and the mission failing? It would be important to reach the latter conclusion as rapidly as possible, to repair any problems that are still reparable at that point, or to recognize failure and cut our losses if things are truly beyond hope.

In Afghanistan, the key is to understand how the war is affecting the daily lives of citizens—their sense of security, of opportunity, of hopefulness, of support for NATO and for their own government. To understand this, we need to understand the size, scale, and geographic concentrations of enemy forces on a detailed basis. We also need to track the performance of Afghan security forces—as well as the broader Afghan justice system, including the courts, because creating a sense of stability and of reasonable government rule is crucial. The following additional indicators of progress would also appear very important, at not only the national but the provincial and district levels:

—The level of violence, and if possible the degree to which the enemy initiates violent encounters (if the enemy causes most of them, it suggests that it retains most of the initiative in the conflict).[6]

—Trends on accidental casualties to civilians caused by Afghan or foreign troops in contact with the enemy.

—The specific levels of targeted violence against key individuals—that is, assassinations and kidnappings of prominent persons as well as of security force personnel. A related metric is how many Afghan leaders are willing to live in the areas they govern.

—The views among the Afghan population about the government and its performance (and its corruption levels), about NATO forces, about law and order in their neighborhoods and villages, about their quality of life as well as economic opportunities—and about various resistance movements, to see if the people are still generally opposed to the insurgency. Measuring these things involves public opinion polls; it also involves watching for signs of citizen involvement on matters such as reporting the locations of IEDs before they detonate.[7]

One key point should be made about Afghanistan: although the above list of indicators starts with trends on violence, these are probably not quite as crucial or determinative as they were in Iraq. This point has been underscored by Jeremy Shapiro and Jason Campbell in previous writings, including in a 2009 paper written with one of us (O'Hanlon), a paper from which some of this section is drawn.[8] In Iraq in 2005–06, the violence was literally tearing the country apart, with most estimates averaging about 3,000 civilian fatalities a month. That was bad enough, but another 100,000 people were being driven from their homes every month. In Afghanistan, even today after the worsening of violence over the recent years, estimated civilian fatality levels are roughly comparable to those in Iraq today and only about 10 percent of the levels in Iraq at the peak of that nation's violence. While the first order of business for the surge in Iraq was to reduce the rates of killing and ethnic displacement, in Afghanistan the lower level of violence means that the higher priority is probably state building. To put it another way, while tragic, the overall level of violence in Afghanistan is not so horrible as to be decisive on its own. If we can cap the violence, and the spread of the Taliban, while building up the Afghan state and thereby making possible an eventual NATO exit strategy, we will likely achieve our core goals. Institution building, starting with the security forces and other instruments of law and order, is probably even more important than killing extremists in this war.[9]

In addition, it is not necessarily bad news if the insurgents in Afghanistan respond to the new buildup of U.S. and Afghan forces by dispersing, going to ground, or relocating rather than fighting. We do not need to kill or capture enemy personnel so much as to build up state institutions so that in the future the Afghans can take on the insurgents themselves. Anything that buys us time to strengthen the Afghan government and improve the Afghan economy works to our advantage. Such dynamics could make time an ally of the Afghan government and NATO; in recent years, time has been our enemy, because the general perception of a worsening situation for Afghans eroded support for the government and the international coalition.

HOW LONG WILL IT TAKE?

Using metrics as the basis for structured discussions about progress in Afghanistan, we should be able to gain a sense about the effectiveness of the strategy within about a year to eighteen months after it is fully adopted. That implies late 2010 or early to mid-2011, given that the Obama administration's second major review of strategy was not completed until the fall of 2009. And if it works, we should be able to begin to reduce U.S. and NATO troops more generally by 2012 or 2013.

The years 2010 and early 2011 should be highly indicative of our prospects, for several reasons. For the first time NATO's full forces will have been in place throughout most of an entire year. By contrast, 2009 was a year of gradual buildup—and even once forces arrived in country, it took time for them to establish the combat outposts required to implement a proper population protection strategy. So anyone who was expecting major results in 2009 was being unrealistic. For some aspects of the mission, 2010 and early 2011 will still be somewhat early for assessing progress. But for other aspects, such as the ability of NATO forces to establish a strong presence throughout the country, we should begin to witness the benefits of the new counterinsurgency policy.

In addition, offensive campaigns within counterinsurgency operations take time. In fact, 2009 was partly a story about simply finding the enemy and otherwise improving intelligence gathering and fusion methods that quickly integrate information from multiple sources for a mission that had not received emphasis in these or other areas before the Obama administration. That means 2010 could be the year of the greatest number of NATO offensives. The history of the Iraq war is replete with campaigns, each often taking a month or two, to establish control in this or that river valley, this or that city. A similar campaign plan for Afghanistan began in 2009 but will surely continue into 2010—especially because some insurgents will winter in Pakistan and return to the fight only in the spring, and because General McChrystal's additional forces requested in response to his strategic review of summer 2009 will not arrive in Afghanistan until 2010.

For these reasons, NATO casualty numbers may not go down at all in 2010 and may even continue to rise—but civilian fatality numbers as well as other indicators of the security and well-being of the Afghan population should begin to decline during the year or certainly by 2011. These improvements should be reflected in concrete data on casualties and in public opinion polling about security conditions and related matters.

Finally, it will take time to improve the Afghan security forces. This is not simply a matter of building up their numbers and putting new troops through basic training. In addition, two other key things need to happen. First, units need to obtain real operational experience in the field with Western forces providing mentors—as well as partner units, generally of somewhat smaller size than the Afghan units. Doing these things at the desired pace is only now becoming possible. It was not until the fall of 2009 when the 4th brigade of the 82nd Airborne Division, designed for such purposes, arrived in country. Even with that unit in place, capacity to accelerate training even further is not yet adequate.

According to existing timelines, it will take until late 2010 just to reach interim numerical goals for the Afghan security forces of about 230,000 total personnel. It will take until 2012 or 2013 to reach McChrystal's 400,000 aggregate goal, if the Obama administration ultimately approves it. And while building up the Afghan army and police force in this way, we will need to keep our eye on matters such as the AWOL rate among soldiers and police—which grew from 7 percent in 2008 to 9 percent in 2009. It means little to claim that Afghan security forces have reached a given size if many individuals fail to show up for work or fail to do their jobs once there.[10]

In the course of 2008, about 35,000 Afghan security forces were recruited and trained, and a similar figure was reached in 2009. The new training capacity will allow at least a 50 percent increase in that number, if adequate recruits can be found.[11] Once numerical goals for the army and police are properly adjusted upward, it will take until at least 2012 to recruit and train a full-sized Afghan security force, as noted, and then another one to two years of intensive mentoring before most are ready to operate on their own.

Other improvements in the security forces, beyond recruiting and training, will have to occur in the next few years as well. When necessary, incompetent leaders in the Afghan forces need to be identified by NATO forces as well as by their own superiors and replaced. This too takes time. In Iraq the national police were in very poor shape through 2006, but the firing and replacement of most of their leaders improved the situation drastically during the course of that year.[12] The process of improvement in Afghanistan has already begun, with rank reform occurring largely in 2008, for example (that reform led among other things to a reduction in the number of police generals from 319 to 120 and in the number of colonels from 2,445 to 235, while also creating pay parity between army and police).[13] But it was only in the fall of 2009 that the first wave of NATO trainers and mentors needed to implement this strategy correctly arrived, and only in 2010 will the full complement be in place. Again, the period of 2010 into early 2011 will be the key period to watch.

Do not expect uniform progress during this period. In fact, as Taliban and other resistance forces potentially step up their efforts and their numbers, overall national statistics on attacks and casualties may worsen for much of the year. But in those provinces and districts where enough resources are deployed, we should be able to see progress in the course of the year—in overall security indicators, in the happiness of the population with the government, in citizens' sense of the quality of law and order in their neighborhoods. Progress should be sustainable, moreover, in places where Afghan security forces gradually assume a larger role from NATO forces. And at some point over the course of the year, overall national statistics on attacks, kidnappings, assassinations, safety and usability of roads, and civilian fatalities should improve too. If they do not, something serious will be wrong, and we will have to face that reality directly and honestly. We ask readers to consult www.brookings.edu/afghanistanindex in the course of 2010 and 2011 and beyond for updates on the raw data needed to make these assessments.

How long will large numbers of foreign troops have to stay in Afghanistan? Again, it would be a mistake to set a schedule, but 2012–13 is a reasonable time frame for beginning a U.S. drawdown from Afghanistan. Again, an analogy with Iraq is instructive—the surge began in early 2007 and even at the end of 2009 troops were still only modestly below their pre-surge levels. Higher numbers of forces were needed for almost two years. In Afghanistan, higher numbers will probably be needed for at least three years, given the slower pace that characterizes the strategy (and life in general) there. In early 2009 then Commander General David McKiernan suggested the new force totals might have to be sustained for three or four years, and he was probably right in this prediction.[14]

If economic development strategies are intensified and better resourced, many of their key goals, such as miles of road improved, can be achieved by about 2012 as well. This in turn will help the Afghan government establish greater legitimacy and popularity among its own people, further depriving the insurgency of support.

While commanders and political leaders are reluctant to propose a schedule for fear of being held to it even when circumstances change, the scale and pace of planned military and economic efforts in Afghanistan implies roughly this kind of calendar—major progress sometime in the course of 2010–11, and the potential for a drawdown to begin around 2012–13. If these developments do not occur, we need to rethink first principles. But we also need to remember the importance of not creating artificial precision in our timelines—or giving the enemy a clear sense of how long we will endure. This chapter's time estimates should thus be seen as notional and approximate, not fixed and binding.

Economic Activity and Land Use in Afghanistan

Legend:
- Irrigated cultivation
- Mixed dry farming and grazing
- Forest
- Sparse vegetation
- ⊙ Capital
- ○ Major city

0 — 100 Miles

- ◗ Oilfield
- ◖ Gasfield
- Fe Iron deposit
- Cu Copper deposit
- U Uranium deposit
- ◊ Oil/gas potential

- Cement plant
- Cotton gin
- Textile plant
- Electric power plant
- Food processing plant

Countries/places labeled: CHINA, TAJIKISTAN, Northern Areas, INDIA, Srinagar, Jammu, ISLAMABAD, Peshawar, PAKISTAN, DUSHANBE, Talogan, Khanabad, Kunduz, Baghlan, Pul-e-Khumri, Charikar, Jalalabad, KABUL, Gardez, Ghazni, Bamyan, Mazar-e Sharif, Balkh, Termiz, UZBEK-ISTAN, Arghandab Dam, Kandahar, Quetta, Kajaki Dam, Lashkar Gah, Zaranj, Farah, Herat, Mary, TURKMENISTAN, IRAN, AFGHANISTAN

CHAPTER SIX

Improving the Strategy

For all its strengths, and for all the improvement of the last two years, current strategy in Afghanistan still has major problems. Not all need to be fixed, or at least fixed promptly, for our core strategic goals—containing the insurgency while helping the Afghan government develop the tools to continue doing so itself—to be achieved. But some are still rather urgent. And on other matters, we should continue to try to set the stage for longer-term progress.

The economy is failing most of the people of the country, even if GDP is growing. Opium remains the backbone of far too much economic activity, with pervasive corrupting effects on society and on the police. International aid and development efforts remain unfocused, with a cacophony of voices and a hodgepodge of specific projects and programs overwhelming the Afghan government's ability to coordinate and control. The Pakistan sanctuary remains a huge Achilles' heel in defeating the Taliban and related militias. The Taliban is a very capable enemy and targets security forces as well as government officials effectively. Improvements in strategy are still needed—and without further delay. The odds are with us in Afghanistan, but the hour is late, and the chances for failure real, so we must not waste any more time.[1] We organize our ideas for improving the current strategy into two categories, security and economics.

SECURITY POLICY PROPOSALS

Some of the following ideas are already being actively debated by Afghan and NATO officials. Others should be.

Further Enlarge and Properly Equip the Afghan Security Forces

Recent NATO and Afghan strategy has emphasized increasing the size of available security forces of all major types. American forces now number 68,000 troops, headed toward a total of around 100,000 in 2010; all together international military personnel exceed 100,000 in all and will probably reach 140,000. Within another year, the Afghan army is projected to reach about 134,000 and the national police, 96,000, for a total security force of 230,000. But this leaves combined forces at just 60 percent or so of the totals recommended by counterinsurgency doctrine—admittedly a rough guide, but still an important one.

Afghan officials themselves, including Defense Minister Wardak, have already argued for an Afghan national army of at least 200,000.[2] The figures of 240,000 army and 160,000 police, as calculated by ISAF, make sense and should be adopted until the insurgency is defeated. Getting more southern Pashtun into the force is important, too.[3]

Establishing force goals of this size would allow foreign countries to plan their security aid appropriately.[4] General Petraeus estimates the cost of Afghan National Security Forces at $10 billion a year, so serious planning is needed. Setting such force goals also would allow recruiting efforts to be properly scaled within Afghanistan. If it is determined that necessary recruiting targets for a larger security force cannot be met, then the government can turn to consideration of military conscription instead. Proper force goals also send a message that we are collectively serious about this mission and doing all that it takes to succeed.

Any increase in army (and police) personnel needs to be accompanied by a parallel effort to strengthen the ministries that oversee them. It is these ministries that monitor possible corruption, ensure prompt payment and other good treatment of personnel, create logistical support, and maintain the command chain. Strengthening these ministries will require embedding more mentors within them.[5] Whenever possible, the mentors should be Afghans themselves—perhaps from abroad where possible— although a certain number of properly chosen Western mentors may be useful too. (This is particularly so if committed individuals can be found who might be willing to do more than a single tour in Afghanistan, paralleling General McChrystal's emphasis on establishing dedicated country experts among his top advisers—individuals who remain focused on the mission even when on rotation back home, and who return to the same part of Afghanistan tour after tour when deployed abroad.)

The quality of the Afghan police also matters. Many police today are illiterate, among their other weaknesses. As salaries and benefits are improved, making service in the army and police more appealing (with monthly pay starting around $240 in combat zones), demands can be increased too, so that a higher-quality force is built over time. Obligatory literacy training is one such requirement that should be introduced as soon as practical. Indeed, emphasizing literacy would presumably have substantial appeal to many Afghans, giving them additional skills needed for the future. As such, it would represent an additional benefit as well as a quality enhancement tool. Ideas like this—which treat the security forces as an elite institution, the way some other nations in the region do, which take care of committed personnel for the duration of their careers and indeed their lives—can also help greatly with the quality of personnel who join and stay in the army and police. Improvements in the quality of the security forces can also be one example of a way in which Afghan national confidence, so damaged after thirty years of war and dependency, can be gradually restored—by giving the nation signature institutions that all can view with patriotic pride.

Some scholars ask whether the U.S. political system is reliable enough to commit funds to an enlarged Afghan security force over an extended period. The answer is yes. The United States has proven as much over the years in funding Egypt, Greece, Israel, South Korea, Taiwan, and Turkey for multiple decades when core U.S. security interests dictated it. Certainly Afghanistan, where al Qaeda once had its main home, is worth a comparable financial investment.

Reform the National Police and the Justice Systems

The police force is one of the key weaknesses of Afghanistan today, and one of the key sources of vulnerability in the current strategy for stabilizing the country. Some of the problems involve top-level policy. Others involve reforms and replacements of specific individuals. There are limits to what the international community can do in promoting reform in this, and other, Afghan institutions. Much must be done by Afghans themselves, and that represents a key vulnerability in our strategy, given the weaknesses of the Karzai regime. But there are some things we can do.

Under the right circumstances, a national police force could avoid the kinds of corrupting influences that currently characterize most of the Afghan police today, where local police are often tied in with local drug runners and other illicit elements of the economy. But the only organization with such a role, the Afghan National Civil Order Police, with well-trained multiethnic units, had only 2,500 trained personnel as of early 2009. Citizens reportedly prefer to deal with this national force because it is not corrupt, but it is badly undersized and needs strengthening as well as enlarging.[6]

How will we know if we are making progress with the Afghan police in the future? Citizen surveys can tell us something, but are not sufficient themselves. It is hard to accurately measure improvement in a country's security forces. In Iraq we trained and equipped Iraqi security forces—at a more vigorous pace in 2004–06 than before—and yet the strategy did not work. In effect, we were equipping them for *contributing to* sectarian warfare rather than stopping it, because the units were heavily infiltrated by extremists who often supported militias and criminals rather than opposing them. Metrics focused on equipment and training cannot easily gauge this kind of fundamental political problem. We must remember this lesson from Iraq. We must further understand that when American or NATO officers help train a unit over a period of time, they can develop a vested interest in scoring it more highly on readiness scales, whether or not the score is correct in a given case. An independent person or organization may therefore have to be involved in the assessment process to give it greater impartiality and accuracy.[7]

Similar concerns apply in Afghanistan. In the case of the Afghan police, problems of reliability and politics may have more to do with the drug trade than with sectarian or insurgent conflict per se. Corruption is a huge challenge. For example, a Canadian newspaper investigation implicated a deputy minister in the Afghan government—the very person responsible for counternarcotics efforts—for protecting drug runners in 2009.[8]

In any event, those employing metrics need to avoid the temptation to document gradual improvements in capacity and training as a mechanical, linear process. In fact, only when units are tested in the field can we really have confidence in them, and to be successful in the field, many will require new leadership and new police cadres, just as proved necessary in Iraq.

To deal with the problem of corruption, Westerners need to develop dossiers on officials suspected of corruption. If they do not, when they report their concerns to Afghan officials, the latter may be tempted to ignore the problem out of fear of challenging a friend or relative or political ally. Only if evidence is incontrovertible will the officials in some cases be convinced to fire those who are impeding reform and fostering a culture of criminality. Sarah Chayes also suggests the creation of committees of redress for local citizens. These would effectively be ombudsmen organizations, designed to compensate citizens cheated out of money by the government and to forward information about government malfeasance to Kabul, where action could be taken if evidence against a given government official or organization became compelling.[9] Still, eradicating bribery from the culture of government in Afghanistan will take time and will have to happen at the instigation of Afghans themselves rather than outsiders. Outside actors can help, first by reducing their own contributions to the problem, since they often reward the very companies and organizations that are corrupt. But the society in general, and its ethos, will have to be repaired before fundamental change can occur. The work of certain reformers in government today shows the way ahead and proves that progress is possible.

The difficulty in finding good, honest, competent leaders may shape how we try to structure Afghan security forces. It may make sense to try to build forces that put more individual soldiers and police under a given commander. This can be done, for example, by "thickening" units—putting more companies within a given battalion, within reason of course, and more battalions within a given brigade, for example.

To deal with the need to make the police larger and more competent, it is also important to stay focused on financial basics. Police reform will not work unless police are adequately paid and equipped and their families provided with survivor benefits should they die on the job, as many already have. Death benefits should not be modest one-time "sympathy payments," but rather sustained support for families who have lost a major breadwinner.[10] Better benefits and pay were approved by the Afghan parliament in late 2009 and must now be funded.

Law and order is not just about the police. Courts need to work too, as do detention capabilities. Afghanistan needs younger judges and more female judges (as of mid-2009, the number of female judges was just 70 out of 1,100 total judges nationwide).[11] Women are probably more difficult to bribe, given the nature of the culture, so should be employed more frequently.

In addition, while court capacity remains limited, a temporary justice system might try to employ tribal shuras to settle normal civil suits concerning property disputes and the like—reserving courts for criminal cases, unless a party to the traditional approach objects. Intermediate approaches may also be worth considering. For example, in Afghanistan in the 1920s, "courts of reconciliation" were created to act as arbiters of disputes. This system could be recreated, with less formality and need for formal legal training among officials than the normal court system would require. Again, any necessary appeals could be made to the formal court—though in many cases, individuals who are illiterate, unimpressed by formal court proceedings, distrustful of the state, or unwilling to endure long delays before gaining access to an official court might prefer the semiofficial approach.[12]

The goal of a proper and state-run justice system should be pursued over time; the hybrid model risks reinforcing tribal systems that are unfair to women and otherwise problematic. It may be a necessary interim measure, but even in such cases, some level of state supervision should be accorded the informal justice sector. As one example, law students might be asked to spend a semester (or a summer) away from their formal studies supervising elders or government functionaries handling certain cases. Students could encourage respect for the proper use of evidence and the concept of basic rights for all citizens.

A Broader Anticorruption Agenda

In addition to improving the army, police, and courts, Afghanistan needs a more concerted strategy for reducing corruption in government ranks more generally.

Planning for better anticorruption strategies has been in the works for months. An anticorruption plan should include the following elements, among others:

—Greater use and coordination of American intelligence assets to develop portfolios on the illicit activities of key Afghan officials, which can then be shared with President Karzai.

—Hardball tactics by the international community in dealing with corrupt officials, depriving them of some or all development funds and asking Afghan central authorities to do the same, as President Obama discussed in his December 1, 2009, speech.

—Ombudsmen at the district, provincial, and national levels to handle citizen complaints against corrupt officials. This tactic will not always work, because corrupt officials are often powerful people who intimidate, but even partial progress would be worth the effort.

—Police force anticorruption task forces with members paid directly by the Ministry of the Interior (to limit the ability of local chiefs to suppress results).

—An independent board to review the performance of provincial governors so that the Afghan president cannot fire them without cause. Of course, such a board could itself be corruptible, so no one method like this is a panacea, but Afghanistan today could probably benefit from more checks and balances—and from more transparency in government decisionmaking.

Corruption cannot be eliminated from Afghanistan. But it can be reduced, and the most egregious cases punished. Such actions would change the atmosphere of impunity that currently prevails and would address the anger that many Afghan citizens feel toward their own government. It is also important to ensure that major tribal groupings do not feel excluded from the benefits of state largesse; to date the Durrani tribal confederation and certain tribes within it friendly to the president are seen as benefiting more than many Ghilzai tribes, for example.

President Karzai is right that Afghanistan needs a "big tent" involving many individuals, and that a certain amount of forgiveness for past transgressions can help create the right spirit of reconciliation. But the current approach has gone too far in the direction of leniency for ongoing, not just past, corruption and other transgressions. It also is characterized by far too much favoritism—embittering those who do not benefit, and making them likely recruits for the insurgency. Improvements are needed, and now.

Think Creatively about Countering IEDs

There is little need to tell soldiers and Marines about the importance of using every tool at our disposal to defeat improvised explosive devices (IEDs). They have been very lethal in Afghanistan, even though Iranian-style explosively formed penetrators (shaped charges that form molten slugs capable of penetrating many kinds of armor) have generally not appeared on the battlefield as they did in Iraq. In Afghanistan, instead, the problem has been somewhat different—culverts under roads that can be packed with huge amounts of conventional explosive that can destroy even MRAPs (mine-resistant, ambush-protected vehicles), or small unpaved country roads where it is easy to bury explosives.

The military's basic approach to tackling IEDs—go after them at every stage, ideally before they can be deployed or even built—is generally sound. But some new ideas may still be needed, beginning with the fact that smaller MRAPs are needed for some Afghan roads and will have to be bought. Afghan security forces also need MRAPs of their own despite the cost; there is no reason not to provide these in large numbers.

Beyond such steps, we would advocate several more. First, greater fixed surveillance of roads might make sense, including infrared cameras for nighttime use. Many checkpoints have been built along various highways. However, for example, on the way to Ghazni or Wardak, police officers leave the checkpoints as the sun sets. These checkpoints are among the enemy's main targets. It is of course unrealistic to put cameras everywhere, but disguising their location could keep insurgents guessing about where they are located. If insurgents become fearful that they might be seen emplacing IEDs—and then attacked—their ability to lay multiple IEDs quickly and fearlessly may be compromised. In addition, ISAF and Afghan forces should do more patrolling and even ambushing at sites where insurgents are known to like to emplace IEDs; this will be a benefit of more forces.

Second, unmanned robotic MRAPs could make sense, to confuse the enemy about which vehicle in a convoy had people inside. Even if this tactic were effective only one out of every three or four times, it would save lives. To be sure, it would cost money and fuel, but given the alternative, that is a small price to pay. For those who would dismiss the idea out of hand, it is worth remembering that the U.S. president is transported in a convoy of two helicopters for just this reason.

Do Reconciliation Right

As noted before, efforts to compromise with the Taliban have not worked and are highly unlikely to work. For these sorts of reasons, most experts like Mohammad Masoom Stanekzai, vice chairman of the Afghan government's Demobilization and Reintegration Commission, focus instead on the grass-roots level. They ask whether lower-level Taliban or other types of less committed insurgents, many of whom may be motivated more by money and other such pragmatic matters than by ideology, can be talked into joining the political process.[13]

One path toward reconciliation is to reach out to citizens in general and try to give them incentives to work with the Afghan government. If successful, this tactic will persuade some former insurgents to lay down their arms and convince other Afghans not to join the insurgency in the first place. This process might be called "indirect reconciliation" and is a more promising and more logical approach than trying to persuade "moderate Taliban" to change sides in the war. The Afghan government is making some efforts along these lines through efforts like the Social Outreach Program of the Independent Directorate of Local Government. Such initiatives help districtwide communities, consisting typically of many small towns and villages, to organize and then provide them with funds for development if they do so successfully. The key to the success of this approach, particularly in a traditional and tribal place such as Afghanistan, is for authorities to recognize the centrality of working with the community, rather than focusing just on the choices and opportunities of the individual.[14]

Reconciliation also can involve giving incentives to individuals and groups that once may have been part of the insurgency, or that might join it in the future, to provide security-related services for the government or the private sector. One pilot program organized by the Afghan government in conjunction with ISAF is known as the Afghan Population Protection Force. It was tried out in Wardak Province near Kabul. The idea requires locals to convene a shura and elect a supervisory council and then to nominate men to be formed into a security group to conduct local patrolling. The group is then trained and monitored by Afghan government officials. A related program known as the Community Defense Initiative works similarly—requiring a community-wide shura and oversight process—but requires less training. In these cases, weapons are generally not provided to the recruits, and funding is provided to the community rather than to the former insurgents directly. Participants are allowed to man checkpoints only within their own communities, and they are obliged to keep hard-core Taliban away if they are to continue qualifying for the benefits of the program.

Even with such conditions, these programs will be difficult to establish in a country where many tribal elders have been killed in recent years and decades. Some NATO allies are also quite nervous about any effort to create semiofficial security structures after so much effort in past years to demobilize militias.[15] But at this point, the mechanisms discussed above do provide many safeguards and other sensitivities to the realities of Afghanistan and should be pursued.[16]

Even less formal approaches may be worth expanding, provided that they do not extend to arming or training militia-like groups. For example, the UN World Food Program contacts local communities to request protection for food deliveries to remote regions. If the communities ensure the food's safety and equitable distribution in their regions, the agency will make the deliveries; otherwise it will not. A major cell phone company in Afghanistan similarly has chosen to pay communities to provide security for its towers rather than hire armed guards, at least in certain rural areas. In some cases, what is really being purchased is loyalty, so that locals do not themselves become the enemy. In yet another model, a local company can be hired to provide certain specific security tasks. The Canadian government, for example, was paying a private Afghan company to help with security around the Kandahar Provincial Reconstruction Team. The Canadians emphasized that the company was credentialed and was not a militia. As a result of the contract, attacks on the base declined dramatically. For each such success story, however, there is a security company (or two) owned by extremists or former warlords, so participants in this kind of effort need to be monitored very carefully.

All these efforts are not necessarily reconciliation per se, because they need not be made with individuals or groups who support the insurgency. But in theory they could include former insurgents, provided that the individuals or groups can be monitored to ensure that their behavior has changed. (Because of the danger of infiltration by unfriendly elements, taking former insurgents into the security forces probably does not make sense—but most other jobs in the government can be offered to those who leave the resistance.) This approach has the added virtue of potentially splitting the enemy—dividing former allies from each other and gaining the help of some in pursuing those insurgents that remain. That creates a multiplier effect. Not only is the size of the opposition reduced, but some former opposition fighters end up supporting the government and NATO. This approach can further disrupt enemy operations by breaking up insurgent forces into pockets of activity rather than a single large area dominated by the resistance.

There will be no broad-based tribal awakening in Afghanistan as there was in Iraq. Tribal groupings are probably not strong or cohesive enough across large areas of the country. Moreover, the Taliban and other militias in Afghanistan have been more careful in their use of force against local citizens than was al Qaeda in Iraq, so the backlash against extremists is not likely to be as great in Afghanistan. But a willingness to create these kinds of partnerships, case by case, even with past enemies provided that their future behavior improves, makes good sense. It should be adopted in more of the country.[17] The key is to remember that the efforts must be carefully monitored and reevaluated frequently to ensure that widespread abuses are not occurring; when they do happen, offending groups should lose their revenue from the government as well as their immunity from possible attack by the army, police, or ISAF units.

Aid Pakistan's Counterinsurgency Efforts

Current U.S. strategy focuses appropriately on the Afghanistan-Pakistan theater as an integrated, interlinked battle space and recognizes that we must work very hard to help the Pakistani government address its own terrorism and insurgency problem. But beyond sustaining the cooperation with Pakistan, and increasing aid as has already been proposed, additional steps and additional brainstorming may be needed.

The Pakistan sanctuary problem is a serious challenge to Afghanistan. Seth Jones of RAND has tabulated a number of cases of past civil wars in which an insurgency had assistance from the outside. When it had direct help from a foreign government, insurgencies won fifteen out of twenty-nine wars and achieved partial success in another six. When an insurgency had substantial outside support from nonstate groups—and the Taliban and other Afghan militias certainly have at least that—insurgencies won eight of twenty-five campaigns and achieved some of their goals in another eight. (By comparison, governments won eleven out of eighteen wars that Jones studied when the insurgency did not have outside help.)[18]

In fact, the Taliban insurgents still appear to enjoy some direct help today from elements of the Inter-Services Intelligence Directorate of the Pakistani Army. The ISI may view the Taliban as a useful hedge in case the current war effort fails, allowing Pakistan to ensure a government friendly to its interests in Afghanistan at that time.[19]

Part of this dynamic is the unfortunate legacy of a Pakistani state that has long viewed insurgent groups, even those willing to use brutal and terrorist methods, as worthy partners. In addition to wanting to avoid an India-friendly government in Kabul, Pakistan has also used its proxies in Afghanistan to train extremist fighters intended ultimately for operations in Kashmir. To the extent that Pakistan is beginning to change its views toward terror as the essence of its own state is threatened by some of the movements, the situation may change. But that will surely take time. Even today, Pakistan is much more apt to target what it considers either Pakistani Taliban or Arab fighters in its midst and disinclined to attack Afghan Taliban or groups like Lashkar-e-Tayyiba (which are often asked to rename themselves, given a short period of penitence after a major attack against India, and then effectively rehabilitated).[20]

Stanford professor Steve Stedman's important work on ending internal wars reaches conclusions similar to those of Jones. Overall his focus is more on conflicts ended by negotiated accords than on wars in process—but his work on why peace accords sometimes fail is still relevant, for it highlights the fault lines in these kinds of conflicts. He identifies three main sources of a renewal of warfare—spoils, spoilers, and hostile neighbors.[21] Spoils are riches such as diamonds, of which Afghanistan has relatively modest amounts, although its capacity for opium production may play a similar destabilizing role in some ways. Spoilers of course are dedicated foes of any peace accord, and Afghanistan would seem to have those in spades. Finally, hostile neighbors are a major problem, and they are what is at issue here. If Pakistan does take its own insurgency problem, as well as Afghanistan's, seriously in the coming years, this concern will be mitigated. But again, Stedman's research highlights the inherent dangers to Afghanistan if that does not occur. Afghanistan has one huge advantage over most of the cases in Stedman's study—the large number of international resources being devoted to its problems.

To address the sanctuary problem more effectively, three more initiatives may be useful to consider, beyond the welcome and overdue military operations that Pakistan has carried out in 2009. First, an "EZ pass" system could be created to facilitate and regulate movement of vehicles and people at main crossings along the Afghanistan-Pakistan border. This would not stop all infiltration, but it would tend to facilitate legitimate flows and thereby free authorities to try to counter illicit flows, pushing more of them to remote regions where it would be harder to move weaponry as well as large numbers of fighters. Second, political reforms should be made in Pakistan's Federally Administered Tribal Areas—Seth Jones suggests lifting the strict regulations on political parties there (which effectively cede turf to extremist religion-based organizations) as well as possibly incorporating the region more formally and normally into Pakistan's polity.[22] Third, greater economic development efforts should be made in the tribal areas—followed by tracking public opinion to know how the population feels about these kinds of efforts and their success. Such tracking can help identify those parts of a strategy that are working and those that are not and allow adjustment in policy as needed.

Lobby Pakistan to Disband the Quetta Shura

It remains a huge paradox that, even as Pakistan and the United States collaborate against some common enemies today, even as Pakistan allows American logistics operations to traverse its territory en route to Afghanistan, even as American aid to Pakistan grows rapidly from its typical recent levels of $1 billion or so a year, Pakistan continues to aid and abet enemy forces. The most blatant way in which this continues is through the country's ongoing tolerance of the so-called Quetta shura. This is the headquarters of the Afghan resistance, and much or even most of it resides, meets, and operates from within the capital of Pakistan's Baluchistan Province.

The United States has been right to try to work with Pakistan despite such divided loyalties in Islamabad. Not all officials in Pakistan approve of support for the Quetta shura or other related activities that occur within their territory. In addition, Pakistan has felt betrayed by the United States itself in the past, going back to a cutoff of arms sales in both the 1970s and 1990s, and as a result it has felt it must hedge its strategic bets. The Taliban represent a pro-Pakistan group that could again seize power within Afghanistan, ensuring that a government relatively friendly to Islamabad would run that country if the NATO mission fails and the current Afghan government crumbles. Given Pakistan's worries about having two troubled fronts, one along the border with India and the other to its north and west, some of this tolerance for the Taliban was probably unavoidable—at least within elements of the ISI. This Pakistani interest in maintaining "strategic depth" in the direction of Afghanistan is militarily unnecessary. But it has had considerable sway in Pakistani strategic and political circles nonetheless.

However, the situation can change with time. As the years pass, as U.S. aid to Pakistan increases and is sustained, as American unmanned aerial vehicles kill extremist Pakistani leaders like Beitullah Mehsud, as top American military officials and civilian leaders build up relationships with Pakistani counterparts, a truer security partnership becomes possible. It will not be realistic to expect that each and every pro-Taliban element of Pakistan's ISI will abandon support for that group. However, it may be possible to ask Pakistan to place the Quetta shura under a form of house arrest. By limiting the activities of this group, and perhaps dispersing its members throughout the country, Pakistan could save NATO and Afghan lives and give us a better chance to win the war. If the U.S. commitment to Afghanistan wavers in the future, Pakistan will always have the option of allowing the Quetta shura to reconstitute so that a friendly regime will again have the means to seize power in Kabul as well as southern and eastern parts of Afghanistan. Over time, this kind of deal should be increasingly reasonable to consider—or at least discuss—among American and Pakistani counterparts, and every effort should be made in that direction.

Plan for an Alliance with Afghanistan

Senator Joseph Lieberman, scholar Ashley Tellis, and others have argued that the United States should establish a formal alliance with Afghanistan to clarify the resoluteness of its security commitments. They believe such an alliance would take away any doubt—from tribal leaders in southern Afghanistan, from the ISI in Pakistan, and from others who continue to hedge their bets—about the country's long-term future. This could make them more inclined to support the central government in Kabul and the NATO security mission.[23]

This argument is generally persuasive, though it is still a bit early to act on it. For one thing, the United States has had formal security commitments in this part of the world before, most notably to Pakistan through the CENTO (Central Treaty Organization) alliance early in the cold war era, and they turned out not to be particularly decisive commitments. The United States, for example, did not directly intervene militarily to support Pakistan in the 1971 war against India. We do not mean to criticize past U.S. policy here; rather, the point is to underscore that entering into a treaty does not automatically create a perception of complete and firm commitment by the United States. Second, at this point it is premature to ask the American citizen, taxpayer, and soldier to commit to the long-term security of a country that needs to prove its own steadfastness first. Afghanistan needs to improve its governance and its security forces and continue to establish order within its own state before a security accord makes sense. And formal alliances do not necessarily help much in defeating insurgencies; the Vietnam war is a case in point.

As such, we would favor such an accord but only after the tide has begun to turn on the battlefield.

ECONOMIC POLICY PROPOSALS

Although we have argued throughout the book that security and associated needs for law and order should be the preeminent concern of Afghan and NATO forces, the economy is important too. Improvements in the economy in the early years after the fall of the Taliban are largely what explained the popularity of the Karzai government and of NATO forces in that earlier period. Since the support of the population is crucial to success in any counterinsurgency, it is important to recreate this sense of economic momentum and of job creation.

Expand Resources for Economic Assistance and Channel Aid through Kabul but with Oversight

Because of the ongoing conflict, our development strategy for Afghanistan should differ from normal approaches to less developed states. For one thing, development efforts should be better designed to build up the authority and credibility of the state.[24] Of course, every legitimate government wants to be respected and appreciated by its own citizens, but in counterinsurgency operations, this goal is even more important because popular support of the government is crucial to defeating the insurgency. If the government is accepted, the insurgency is deprived of its chief claim for trying to overturn it. Insurgencies most often succeed where citizens are disaffected with their own government to the point of being willing to use force; counterinsurgencies succeed when they can defuse such anger and garner support for the state instead. This means working through the government on development projects whenever feasible, as the British government and others have advocated. Even if a nongovernmental organization (NGO) or another actor disburses the aid or oversees the development effort—and indeed this will often be necessary, given the limited capacity and in some cases the corruption of the central government—the Afghan government should be credited as much as possible with playing a role. It already has a National Development Strategy guiding its efforts, which is appropriate; it might also create an independent development advisory board made up of Afghans abroad and at home to provide additional oversight and ideas.

Part of Senator Lieberman's wise suggestion for a "civilian surge" in Afghanistan to go along with the military buildup should accordingly emphasize greater support for Afghan ministries, including placing expatriate Afghans and foreign experts within those ministries.[25] There may be value in involving not only Westerners, but Indians, Pakistanis, Turks, Bangladeshis, and Malaysians where possible. They understand the culture and certainly the religion better than do most Americans; they may also be less conspicuous targets for terrorist attacks; many may also cost less. However, as General Petraeus has noted, given available constraints on civilian capacity, it may be more realistic to think of any type of such "surge" as a gradual but sustained civilian increase.[26]

In addition, salaries for government employees must be reasonably high, so that state institutions can be built up. This is important because the huge number of foreign contractors and troops in the country creates many jobs with unusually high pay scales for Afghans—enticing many of them who are needed in government to leave public service and instead work for foreigners. In developing countries that are not in conflict, it is important not to make public service so appealing that private entrepreneurship is discouraged. In the long-term this is true for Afghanistan as well, but in the short term, it is important to keep good people in government jobs so that institutions can be strengthened.

There are several other problems with aid to Afghanistan today. One is clearly the difficulty of getting money to the grass-roots level; most U.S. development funds come with too many stipulations about the percentage of monies that must be spent on American personnel or services. In a wartime environment, this is even less justifiable than is normally the case with development aid. A new aid approach should place greater emphasis on developing Afghan firms for tasks such as construction, road building, and provision of utilities rather than relying so heavily on Western organizations.[27] Western contractors have high costs, given the salaries of expatriates—by some estimates up to 40 percent of development funds for Afghanistan end up back in the West for this and related reasons. That is understandable, and necessary, in some cases but to be avoided where possible.[28] In construction projects, an additional advantage of indigenous firms is that by using simpler designs and methods they may create structures that are easier and cheaper to maintain over the long term.

Of course, in the process, corruption must be checked. Subcontracting can be a major problem, because it leads to multiple "finder fees" paid to multiple firms as the subcontracting process plays out. So subcontracting needs to be better supervised or even banned.

In addition, more effort needs to go into ensuring that a wider spectrum of tribal groupings (especially from the Ghilzai tribal grouping, which provides the core of Taliban support) benefit from the contracting process to avoid the current perception of favoritism.[29] Naturally, we need to have good enough intelligence on various key individuals to reduce the risks of Ghilzai contractors' using their profits to fund the Taliban—but this is precisely the kind of intelligence that coalition forces are now working hard to obtain. Special efforts should also be made to include women of all sectarian groups and tribal backgrounds in various projects and contracts. These types of efforts to work with Afghan organizations should also extend to Afghan NGOs.

It also makes sense for foreign forces to buy more local content—such as bottled water and fresh produce—than is currently the case. Pilot efforts have shown that these measures can be adopted safely, and National Defense University scholars Andrew Mara and Lynn McGrath have offered ideas for further reassurances. Expanding local purchasing could inject another $1 billion a year into the local economy, including in places where it could offer viable alternatives to opium by encouraging crop farming.[30]

It might also be a good idea to require expatriates to pay taxes to Afghanistan on money they earn in the country, as Peter Bergen and Sameer Lalwani have suggested. This would increase Afghan government revenues by several hundred million dollars a year without being onerous on foreigners, given Afghanistan's modest personal tax rates. It could also soften the anger some Afghans feel about the nature of the foreign presence in their country.[31]

On the broader subject of private sector development, most programs to date have not been successful in Afghanistan. These programs have been focused on training and, in some cases, on activities such as taking a few Afghan women abroad to learn how to write business plans. But the training is often quite repetitive and clichéd, and the business plans have typically been shelved—like most strategic plans written by the foreign advisers to the various ministries. (For example, the Ministry of Higher Education has twelve strategic plans.) The Afghan business environment today operates in a simpler, word of mouth, pragmatic fashion. Afghans do not typically understand the value of a business plan and will rarely use one. They generally learn only when they are shown how to manage production in a factory rather than through theory and written words.

Paperwork demands for pursuing contracts can also be enormous. Consider one of our experiences (Sherjan's) at her company, called Boumi. The company decided to reply to a request for proposals (RFP) to supply Afghan National Army uniforms. These contracts are paid by the U.S. Army, and so the RFP is sent from the contracting office at the Camp Eggers U.S. army base in Kabul. The fifty-three-page RFP, which had to be completed and returned within two weeks, was extremely complicated, filled with confusing directions and with legalities that were seemingly directed at U.S.-based businesses. Even with the help of American friends in Washington, Sherjan spent countless hours trying to provide pricing and other information that turned out not to be needed. In her view the RFP could have been five pages long and still provided as much information as necessary to let the contract. In any event, the longer forms are not preventing corruption but are simply keeping Afghan companies that could otherwise do the job out of the competition.

Reforms to spur private sector activity, and to improve the access of Afghans to good housing, are also needed. Many of these require work on property rights. As Ashraf Ghani, the country's former finance minister, puts it, "Two decades of war and forced migration have led to multiple claims on the same assets." These will have to be resolved, with new deeds made impervious to counterfeiting and accessible to all through computerized records; losers in disputes will have to be compensated. Ghani also emphasizes the need to follow standard international practices of the Extractive Industry Transparency Initiative to be sure that the country's untapped abundant mineral resources are developed in ways that are fair to the government and people of the country; he estimates that doing so can lead to a quadrupling in overall government revenue within a decade.[32] To be sure, some of the profits are likely to stay with the local government to protect mining operations and compensate locals displaced by them, but the process can and must be regularized, with most profits going to the central government. The international role in such reforms is relatively inexpensive, primarily requiring some expert advice within Afghan ministries and assistance in purchasing computer systems.

Greater emphasis on agriculture, an employment-creating development effort, is also appropriate. If done well, it can also serve as an effective counternarcotics strategy. Such an effort will create the infrastructure needed to deliver fertilizer and seeds to farmers and move crops to market. It could also include construction of new processing and storage facilities in the major cities.[33] Sarah Chayes has proposed a program to give farmers free saplings for orchards as well as payments for the first five years after planting until the trees start to produce cash crops. This approach is designed to compensate for the income they would have received during that time had they continued to grow poppy rather than licit crops.[34]

Tying all of these ideas together is the simple need for more resources. According to Bruce Riedel, the scale of most major efforts in Afghanistan in areas such as education and road building has been roughly one-fourth to one-half of what is needed. It may be hard to double, triple, or quadruple aid flows without worsening problems of waste and corruption, but the international community should be willing to provide substantial targeted aid increases on proven concepts and in cases where overhead costs are contained.

For example, although some 20,000 kilometers of rural access roads have been repaired or built since 2003, and Afghanistan's ring road that circles the country is now nearly 80 percent complete, more than 40,000 kilometers of roads remain in disrepair. As a result, fewer than half of all villages have access to a road for commercial purposes. Current plans would get the figure up to only 65 percent by 2013.[35] Similarly, rehabilitation efforts for irrigation systems are lagging, with plans adequate to cover only half of all needs.[36] An added aid effort in the range of another $1 billion a year from the international community is appropriate.[37] That effort should also attempt to create a multiyear plan for completing key goals (rather than revisiting interim goals yearly), coordinated much more tightly across the multitudes of donors working within Afghanistan today.

Tighten Aid and Appoint a Single, Strong International Coordinator with Authority

In 2008 and 2009, international military command arrangements in Afghanistan were tightened and improved. All foreign forces were placed under a single American commander, now General McChrystal, and McChrystal was assigned a three-star general (Lt. Gen. David M. Rodriguez) to be his operational commander. A similar corrective is needed on the economic and development side.[38]

After three decades of war, most Afghan ministries have no more than a few competent professionals to run their operations. Among other challenges, they must deal with dozens of international donors, whose efforts are uncoordinated and often amount to a hodgepodge of individually worthy but disconnected efforts.[39] Imagine this: if the competent ministers each receive just one briefing a month from each donor and spend time digesting what they have learned, they could easily consume half their precious time just listening to PowerPoint presentations (two briefings a day, every day, plus time to prepare and to process).

We owe our Afghan friends more help. An international aid coordinator, accountable to all major donors and representing a single major point of contact for the Afghan government, should be named. This person should be powerful. But in deference to Afghan sensitivities and prerogatives about sovereignty, he or she should not be a high commissioner with responsibilities beyond aid and economics.[40] In fact, the whole purpose of this coordinator would be to strengthen the Afghan government by routing as much aid as possible through its administrative organs at the federal and subfederal levels. Perhaps the existing U.N. coordinator could assume this role, but if so, he needs to be given much greater stature as first among donor representatives. The U.N. coordinator does not have nearly enough control over most funds to play this role well at present. One of the key jobs of this coordinator would be to push donors to improve their own internal mechanisms for disbursing, and coordinating, aid efforts.[41]

With two-thirds of all foreign forces in Afghanistan American, it is natural that not only the ISAF commander but his deputy in charge of day-to-day operations be U.S. military officers. But with more than half of all economic assistance coming from non-U.S. origins, the aid and development coordinator should probably be European.

Greater international aid coordination could also include a greater role for Afghan NGOs. An organization with a name like "aid watch" might be created to monitor independently the ways in which aid is disbursed and employed within the country. Such an organization could probably be more effective if able to liaise with a single main international contact, the new aid coordinator.

Pursue Bold Trade Initiatives

To build their economy, Afghans first need security and infrastructure. But they also need markets for agricultural goods, gems, minerals, and other exports. A natural market for Afghan agricultural goods is the European Union, for example; yet tariffs and other trade restrictions impede commerce. This should change. The United States should also create a duty-free import system for goods from Afghanistan; bills to move in this direction were introduced in Congress in 2009, but action has been slow.[42]

To kick-start the process in the coming years, NATO might consider leasing some space on its cargo planes returning from delivering supplies to troops to Afghan firms selling produce abroad.[43] Western nations might also buy up excess wheat at higher-than-market prices in years with bumper crops like 2009, so that farmers shifting from opium production will not be discouraged by low prices.

Trade initiatives could also be of huge value in regard to Pakistan, where textile manufacturing is a major industry. But as with Afghan products, trade barriers limit Pakistan's access to U.S. markets. (By contrast with the United States, Afghanistan has a legitimate reason to protect some young industries from imports from neighbors.) Given the security importance of Pakistan, such barriers should be lifted in the United States; there has been movement on this issue in Congress in 2009, but with inconclusive results for the economy of Pakistan.[44] Pakistani businesses should also be given incentives to establish franchises on Afghan soil, paying Afghans for their work and then benefiting from the privileges accorded to Afghanistan to profit from export market opportunities.

Strengthen U.S. Government Civilian Capacity in Afghanistan

As noted, the civilian component of U.S. and NATO efforts in Afghanistan remains underdeveloped. Despite many exhortations, the civilian surge meant to accompany the military buildup in Afghanistan is slow and modest in scale.

One reason for this shortfall is chronic underfunding of the State Department's Office of Reconstruction and Stabilization. There simply are not enough dollars or people available for such efforts. Similarly, the foreign service within State as well as the full-time employees of the Agency for International Development remain understaffed as well. Finally, the U.S. government has no dedicated career path for civilians specializing in stability operations.[45] To some extent, an adequate pool of foreign service officers and development experts would obviate the need for a dedicated group of individuals. But in the absence of such capacity, and in recognition of the special skills associated with provincial reconstruction team (PRT) work, a case can be made for a dedicated specialty and career track as well.

Hiring and training people takes time, of course. That can be discouraging when policy options for an ongoing war are being considered. However, it is not too late to build up capacity. During the early years of the Iraq war, it was tempting to say that there was no need for a larger U.S. Army or Marine Corps presence because we were, after all, on the way out. This was always a bad argument. But because it was slightly less incorrect each year than it had been the year before, it was hard to defeat the argument—until late 2006 and early 2007 when Congress and a new secretary of defense let common sense prevail. We need to do the same thing now, on the civilian side, motivated largely by Afghanistan. Even if a buildup in civilian capacity provides no real added capability for a couple of years, it will help to have more people by 2011–12. In the meantime, we will have to improvise, ask for special sacrifice by those already able to do so, rely on contractors more than we might prefer in some situations, and prioritize where we place our civilians. But that is no reason to fail to take proper steps to create more capacity.

Focusing on the State Department's Office of Stabilization and Reconstruction and related efforts, we should take four steps:[46]

—Establish a larger senior planning team in Washington

—Create a several-hundred-strong response corps that can move out quickly when stabilization missions are needed

—Create a several-thousand-strong government-wide roster of individuals committed to serve when called upon to do so

—Create another several-thousand-strong roster of individuals akin to a military reserve, with previous relevant experience (ranging from police work to Peace Corps to previous PRT assignments), able to be called upon when needed

In the meantime, though, we need to keep the problem in perspective. The mission in Afghanistan will not fail because military officers temporarily perform jobs that, ideally, civilians should carry out, or because models of development activity are different from the norm in other places. Afghanistan is a country at war, and security forces therefore have an inherently important role. Whether PRTs are staffed mostly by military personnel or by a mix of troops and civilians, they will retain a quasi-military character as long as protection is needed for their members. That is simply a reality. PRT members do have to be sensitive to local conditions, attempt to support rather than supplant local government structures, and where possible work themselves out of a job. There may also be times when they should be particularly careful to minimize their presence, their visibility, and their public association with Afghans who could be targeted in response to having had contact with foreigners.[47] But PRTs had some success in Iraq, and they can in Afghanistan as well.

CONCLUSIONS

Afghanistan is a country with a reasonably long history as a nation. The relative lack of sectarian violence and the population's fatigue with three decades of war suggest a real readiness on the part of the Afghan people for building a stable state. Afghans are indeed good fighters, and they are indeed relatively weak on human capital after thirty years of national deterioration—but they are not xenophobes, and the vast majority of them are not extremists. On balance, they will work with the international community to help establish a functioning country; they are not spoiling for a fight or for decades more of chaos and backwardness.

NATO has its challenges as an alliance. But it has shown remarkable resilience in a mission so far from home for all member states, and in a war that has already caused more than 500 fatalities among troops from non-American states. American armed forces have never been better at counterinsurgency.

The sanctuary for fighters and Taliban leaders in Pakistan causes major problems for Afghanistan. But Pakistan finally appears to be taking on this problem, at least to a degree. In addition, especially in southern Afghanistan, the insurgency has depended primarily on local fighters rather than on individuals coming from Pakistan. So if we can make progress in reducing recruits within Afghanistan, while convincing some "accidental guerrillas" to put down their arms, we can make substantial headway even if the Pakistan problem continues at some level. The police are weak in Afghanistan, it is true, but major improvements in the army there shows what is possible if we get the right leadership, incentive structures, and reform programs. Opium production is a big problem, but it need not be eradicated to defeat the insurgency; we need not make Afghanistan crime-free or drug-free to make it relatively cohesive as a state. Poverty remains rampant in the country, but conditions are much better overall than a decade ago, and Afghans know it and like it. They do not want a return to what they had before. Violence is a problem, but civilian fatalities occur at only about one-tenth the rate they did in Iraq before the surge.

We could still lose, and Afghanistan could again fall apart. But measured against a modest standard of success, and if some entirely feasible reforms are made soon by Afghans as well as by the international community, Afghan citizens and their NATO friends and counterparts *should* be able to achieve their core goals. The odds are with us, not against us. It could take until well into 2010 or early 2011 to be sure that our collective approach is working, and a couple more years after that before major force reductions can occur. Serious losses will continue throughout this period, and more lives will be lost. But compared with what Afghanistan has suffered in the past, and compared with what the Western world has suffered at the hands of terrorists with links to Afghan soil, the sacrifice is worth it and better than any alternative. The case for toughing it out in Afghanistan is still very strong.

Notes

CHAPTER ONE

1. Barack Obama, "Remarks by the President on a New Beginning," Cairo University, June 4, 2009 (www.nytimes.com/2009/06/04/us/politics/04obama. text.html?ref=middleeast [June 5, 2009]).

2. Ashraf Ghani, "A Ten-Year Framework for Afghanistan: Executing the Obama Plan . . . and Beyond," Atlantic Council, Washington, D.C., April 2009, p. 1 (www.acus.org [May 25, 2009]).

3. Department of Defense, *Progress toward Security and Stability in Afghanistan, June 2009* (June 2009), p. 34 (www.defenselink.mil/pubs/pdfs/1230_June-2009Final.pdf [November 2009]).

4. Carl Hulse, "Democrats Have Qualms over War in Afghanistan," *New York Times,* April 24, 2009 (www.nytimes.com/2009/04/24/us/politics/24spend. html [June 5, 2009]); Perry Bacon Jr., "Obama, Progressive Democrats to Talk War Funding," *Washington Post online,* April 28, 2009 (http://voices.washingtonpost.com/44/2009/04/28/obama_progressive_democrats_to.html [June 5, 2009]).

5. General Stanley McChrystal, "COMISAF Initial Assessment," unclassified version, *Washington Post,* September 21, 2009 (www.washingtonpost.com/wp-dyn/content/article/2009/09/21/AR2009092100110_pf.html [October 1, 2009]).

6. Peter Bergen, "The Front," *New Republic,* October 19, 2009 (www.tnr.com/print/article/world/the-front [October 29, 2009]).

7. Gordon Smith, "On Afghanistan and the Canadian Interest," *Global Brief: World Affairs in the 21st Century* (May 2009), p. 60 (www.globalbrief.ca.)

8. Sean Rayment, "Army Chief Warns of 'Terrifying Prospect' of Failure in Afghanistan," *London Sunday Telegraph,* October 4, 2009, p. 1.

9. David Rohde, "Held by the Taliban," *New York Times,* October 18, 2009, p. A1, and October 19, 2009, p. A1; Comments of Bruce Riedel at the Brookings Institution, October 16, 2009 (www.brookings.edu/events/2009/1016_Afghanistan_debate.aspx).

10. Steven Simon and Jonathan Stevenson, "Afghanistan: How Much Is Enough?" *Survival* 51, no. 5 (October/November 2009), pp. 47–67; Paul R. Pillar, "Who's Afraid of a Terrorist Haven?" *Washington Post,* September 16, 2009 (www.washingtonpost.com/wp-dyn/content/article/2009/09/15/AR2009091502977.html [October 22, 2009]).

11. A number of scholars have explained this dynamic, but a particularly concise and compelling version is Bruce Riedel, *The Search for al Qaeda: Its Leadership, Ideology, and Future* (Washington: Brookings, 2008), pp. 24–36.

12. Bruce Riedel, "Comparing the U.S. and Soviet Experiences in Afghanistan," *CTC Sentinel* 2, issue 5 (May 2009), p. 2 (www.ctc.usma.edu/sentinel [June 1, 2009]).

13. Seth G. Jones, *In the Graveyard of Empires: America's War in Afghanistan* (New York: W. W. Norton & Co., 2009), p. 160.

14. Government of Canada, "Canada's Engagement in Afghanistan: Report to Parliament" (Ottawa: March 2009), p. 3.

15. Jones, *In the Graveyard of Empires,* p. 237.

16. Ghani, "A Ten-Year Framework for Afghanistan," pp. 13, 19.

17. Max Boot, "There's No Substitute for Troops on the Ground," *New York Times,* October 22, 2009 (www.nytimes.com [October 22, 2009]).

18. International Security Assistance Force, "ISAF Metrics Briefing: June 2009," Kabul, July 8, 2009, provided by personal communication from ISAF headquarters.

19. International Republican Institute, "Afghanistan Public Opinion Survey: July 16–26, 2009," pp. 18, 58 (www.iri.org [August 18, 2009]).

20. Petraeus's zone of responsibility with Central Command includes Pakistan and Afghanistan, as well as Bahrain, Egypt, Iran, Iraq, Jordan, Kazakhstan, Kuwait, Kyrgyzstan, Lebanon, Oman, Qatar, Saudi Arabia, Syria, Tajikistan, Turkmenistan, the United Arab Emirates, Uzbekistan, and Yemen. Until 2008, when the Africa Command was created, CENTCOM also included Djibouti, Eritrea, Ethiopia, Kenya, Somalia, and Sudan. See www.centcom.mil/en/countries/aor [June 3, 2009].

21. Mark Moyar, *A Question of Command: Counterinsurgency from the Civil War to Iraq* (Yale University Press, 2009), pp. 259–61.

22. Josh White, "A Shortage of Troops in Afghanistan," *Washington Post,* July 3, 2008, p. A1.

23. Fred W. Baker III, "Success in Iraq, Afghanistan Critical to Military Way Ahead, Mullen Says," American Forces Press Service News Articles, December 17, 2007 (www.defenselink.mil/news/newsarticle.aspx?id=48436 [June 5, 2009]).

24. Dexter Filkins, "U.S. Toughens Airstrike Policy in Afghanistan," *New York Times,* June 22, 2009 (www.nytimes.com/2009/06/22/world/asia/22airstrikes.html?hp [June 22, 2009]).

25. Michael M. Phillips, "Stalemate," *Wall Street Journal,* May 23, 2009, p. 1.

26. Stephen Biddle, "Assessing the Case for War in Afghanistan," Testimony before the Committee on Foreign Relations, U.S. Senate, September 16, 2009, p. 8 (www.cfr.org [September 20, 2009]); Jason Lyall and Isaiah Wilson, "Rage against the Machines: Explaining Outcomes in Counterinsurgency Wars," *International Organization* 63, no. 1 (Winter 2009), pp. 69–71; Ivan Arreguin-Toft, "How the Weak Win Wars: A Theory of Asymmetric Conflict," *International Security* 26, no. 1 (Summer 2001), pp. 93–128; Andrew J. Enterline and Joseph Magagnoli, "Is the Chance of Success in Afghanistan Better than a Coin Toss?" *Foreign Policy* (Aug. 27, 2009) (www.foreignpolicy.com/articles/2009/08/27/is_the_chance_of_success_in_afghanistan_better_than_a_coin_toss).

27. Tom Coghlan, "The Taliban in Helmand: An Oral History," in *Decoding the New Taliban: Insights from the Afghan Field,* edited by Antonio Giustozzi (Columbia University Press, 2009), p. 146.

28. See, for example, Rajiv Chandrasekaran, "In Kandahar, A Taliban on the Rise," *Washington Post,* September 14, 2009, p. A1; Tim McGirk, "Why the Taliban Is Gaining Ground in Afghanistan," *Time,* September 16, 2009 (www.time.com [October 1, 2009]).

29. Rajiv Chandrasekaran, "In Helmand, A Model for Success?" *Washington Post,* October 22, 2009, p. A1.

30. Carol Graham and Soumya Chattopadhyay, "Well-Being and Public Attitudes in Afghanistan: Some Insights from the Economics of Happiness," Foreign Policy Working Paper 2, Brookings, Washington, D.C., May 2009, p. 9.

31. Ghani, "A Ten-Year Framework for Afghanistan," p. 4; M. Shaw, "Drug Trafficking and the Development of Organized Crime in Post-Taliban Afghanistan," in *Afghanistan's Drug Industry: Structure, Functioning, Dynamics and Implications for Counternarcotics Policy,* edited by D. Buddenberg and W. A. Byrd (Washington: World Bank, 2006), pp. 204–206 (http://siteresources.worldbank.org/SOUTHASIAEXT/Resources/Publications/448813-1164651372704/UNDC.pdf [June 5, 2009]).

32. Ronald E. Neumann, "Afghanistan: Looking Forward," *The Afghanistan Papers, No. 1,* Centre for International Governance Innovation (Waterloo, Ontario: July 2009), p. 8 (www.cigionline.org [July 10, 2009]).

33. Department of Defense, *Progress toward Security and Stability in Afghanistan, June 2009.*

34. Adam B. Ellick, "Running Out of Options, Afghans Pay for an Exit," *New York Times,* July 5, 2009, p. A10.

35. Dexter Filkins, Mark Mazzetti, and James Risen, "Brother of Afghan Leader Is Said to Be on CIA Payroll," *New York Times,* October 28, 2009, p. A1.

36. Jones, *In the Graveyard of Empires,* p. 99.

37. Testimony of Peter Bergen, New America Foundation, before the U.S. House Committee on Oversight and Government Reform's Subcommittee on National Security and Foreign Affairs, March 4, 2009, p. 8.

38. Jones, *In the Graveyard of Empires,* p. 267.

39. Ibid., p. 318.

40. Admiral Michael Mullen, "The Future of Global Engagements and Defense Budget Priorities," Joint Chiefs of Staff speech, May 18, 2009 (www.brookings.edu/~/media/Files/events/2009/0518_mullen/20090518_mullen.pdf [June 1, 2009]).

CHAPTER TWO

1. Stephen Philip Cohen, *The Idea of Pakistan* (Brookings, 2004), p. 14.

2. Barnett R. Rubin, "The Transformation of the Afghan State," in *The Future of Afghanistan,* edited by J. Alexander Their (Washington: U.S. Institute of Peace Press, 2009), pp. 14–15.

3. Ahmed Rashid, *Taliban* (Yale University Press, 2000), pp. 1–13; Joshua T. White, *Pakistan's Islamist Frontier: Islamic Politics and U.S. Policy in Pakistan's North-West Frontier* (Arlington, Va.: Center on Faith and International Affairs, 2008), pp. 23–25.

4. Bruce Riedel, "Comparing the U.S. and Soviet Experiences in Afghanistan," *CTC Sentinel* 2, no. 5 (May 2009), p. 2 (www.ctc.usma.edu/sentinel [June 1, 2009]).

5. Seth G. Jones, *In the Graveyard of Empires: America's War in Afghanistan* (New York: W.W. Norton, 2009), pp. 37–40.

6. Steve Coll, *Ghost Wars: The Secret History of the CIA, Afghanistan, and bin Laden, from the Soviet Invasion to September 10, 2001* (New York: Penguin Books, 2004), pp. 189–92.

7. Seth G. Jones, *Counterinsurgency in Afghanistan* (Santa Monica, Calif.: RAND, 2008), pp. 26–28.

8. Jones, *In the Graveyard of Empires,* p. 47.

9. Jones, *Counterinsurgency in Afghanistan,* pp. 26–27; Stockholm International Peace Research Institute, *SIPRI Yearbook 1995* (Oxford University Press, 1995), pp. 28–35.

10. James F. Dobbins, *After the Taliban: Nation-Building in Afghanistan* (Washington: Potomac Books, Inc., 2008), pp. 1–3. On Pakistan's support for extremism, see Arvin Bahl, *From Jinnah to Jihad: Pakistan's Kashmir Quest and the Limits of Realism* (New Delhi: Atlantic Books, 2007), pp. 3662.

11. Seth G. Jones, "The Rise of Afghanistan's Insurgency: State Failure and Jihad," *International Security* 32, no. 4 (Spring 2008), p. 12.

12. One aspect of this constitution is the degree of power entrusted in the central government, including the president's right to hire and fire governors. As one manifestation of this, between late 2007 and mid-2009, Karzai replaced more than 80 percent of Afghanistan's thirty-four governors. See Department of Defense, *Progress toward Security and Stability in Afghanistan, June 2009* (June 2009), p. 43 (www.defenselink.mil/pubs/pdfs/1230_June-2009Final.pdf [November 2009]).

13. Much of this is drawn from Jason Campbell, Michael O'Hanlon, and Jeremy Shapiro, "Assessing Counterinsurgency and Stabilization Missions," Foreign Policy Paper 14 (Brookings, May 2009); and Michael E. O'Hanlon and Adriana Lins de Albuquerque, "Afghanistan Index" (Brookings, February 23, 2005 (www.aed.usace.army.mil/faqs/Afghanistan%20Index.pdf [June 22, 2009]).

14. United Nations Office on Drugs and Crime, "Afghanistan Opium Survey 2008: Executive Summary," (Vienna: August 2008), p. 19.

15. International Crisis Group, *Afghanistan: The Need for International Resolve* (Brussels: February 2008), pp. ii, 5.

16. Jeffrey A. Dressler, "Securing Helmand: Understanding and Responding to the Enemy," Afghanistan Report 2 (Washington: Institute for the Study of War, September, 2009, p. 7 [www.understandingwar.org]).

17. Joanna Nathan, "Reading the Taliban," in *Decoding the New Taliban: Insights from the Afghan Field,* edited by Antonio Giustozzi (Columbia University Press, 2009), p. 37; Mohammad Osman Tariq Elias, "The Resurgence of the Taliban in Kabul, Logar, and Wardak," in *Decoding the New Taliban,* edited by Giustozzi, p. 54.

18. General Stanley A. McChrystal, "COMISAF Initial Assessment," unclassified version, *Washington Post,* September 21, 2009 (www.washingtonpost.com/wp-dyn/content/article/2009/09/21/AR2009092100110_pf.html [October 1, 2009]).

19. Ashraf Ghani, "A Ten-Year Framework for Afghanistan: Executing the Obama Plan . . . and Beyond" (Washington: Atlantic Council, April 2009), pp. 1–3 (www.acus.org [May 25, 2009]).

20. Greg Jaffe, "'Almost a Lost Cause,'" *Washington Post,* October 4, 2009, p. A1; Joshua Partlow and Greg Jaffe, "Deadly Attack by Taliban Tests New Strategy," *Washington Post,* October 5, 2009, p. A1.

21. Liaison Office of the Netherlands, "Three Years Later: A Socio-Political Assessment of Uruzgan Province from 2006 to 2009," Kabul, September 18, 2009, p. 22 (www.tlo-afghanistan.org [October 3, 2009]), p. 22.

22. Sarah Chayes, *The Punishment of Virtue: Inside Afghanistan after the Taliban* (New York: Penguin Books, 2006), pp. 84–102; see also McChrystal, "COMISAF Initial Assessment."

23. Liaison Office of the Netherlands, "Three Years Later: A Socio-Political Assessment of Uruzgan Province from 2006 to 2009," p. 28.

24. Obaid Younossi and others, *The Long March: Building an Afghan National Army* (Santa Monica, Calif.: RAND, 2009), pp. 15, 19, 22–23, 30–32, 38–39, 57; see also Combined Security Transition Command-Afghanistan, "The Enduring Ledger," May 2009 (www.cstc-a.com [June 2, 2009]).

25. For one sobering account of the situation, see Matthieu Aikins, "The Master of Spin Boldak," *Harper's Magazine* (December 2009), pp. 52–62.

26. Judy Dempsey, "German General Breaks Silence on Afghanistan," *International Herald Tribune*, November 30, 2008.

27. U.S. Department of Defense News Briefing with Major General Robert Cone, November 12, 2008.

28. International Crisis Group, *Afghanistan: The Need for International Resolve*, p. 7.

29. Michael J. McNerney, "Stabilization and Reconstruction in Afghanistan: Are PRTs a Model or a Muddle?" *Parameters* (Winter 2005–2006), p. 38 (www. carlisle.army.mil/usawc/Parameters/05winter/mcnernet.pdf [May 1, 2009]).

30. Subcommittee on Oversight and Investigations, Committee on Armed Services, U.S. House of Representatives, "Agency Stovepipes vs. Strategic Agility: Lessons We Need to Learn from Provincial Reconstruction Teams in Iraq and Afghanistan," U.S. Congress, April 2008, p. 13 (armedservices.house.gov/pdfs/Reports/PRT_Report.pdf [May 1, 2009]).

CHAPTER THREE

1. For a good summary, see Ashley J. Tellis, *Reconciling with the Taliban? Toward an Alternative Grand Strategy in Afghanistan* (Washington: Carnegie Endowment for International Peace, 2009), p. 16.

2. Seth G. Jones, *In the Graveyard of Empires: America's War in Afghanistan* (New York: W. W. Norton & Co., 2009), pp. 228, 266.

3. Helene Cooper and Eric Schmitt, "White House Debate Led to Plan to Widen Afghan Effort," *New York Times,* March 28, 2009 (www.nytimes.com/2009/03/28/us/politics/28prexy.html?_r=1&scp=7&sq=march%2028%20 afghanistan&st=cse [May 29, 2009]).

4. Testimony of Peter Bergen, New America Foundation, before the U.S. House Committee on Oversight and Government Reform's Subcommittee on National Security and Foreign Affairs, March 4, 2009, p. 4.

5. We also need to avoid a myopic focus on Osama bin Laden and other top al Qaeda leaders. As Audrey Kurth Cronin has shown in a detailed historical study, terrorist groups generally are defeated in one of four ways. Killing or capturing leaders, our apparent strategy according to Mr. Obama's rhetoric, is indeed one possibility. But it does not always work. Defeating a movement more generally and systematically—through a concerted and comprehensive military campaign—is another method. A third possibility involves persuading parts of

a terrorist movement to engage politically rather than through violence. And a fourth approach entails eliminating the popular support for the movement. This is another way of saying that we are better served by a broad-based approach that attacks terrorist networks in various ways—which means creation of a stronger Afghan state, if the other approaches are also to be attempted. See Audrey Kurth Cronin, *Ending Terrorism: Lessons for Defeating al-Qaeda,* Adelphi Paper 394 (London: International Institute for Strategic Studies, 2008), pp. 28-49.

6. Sarah Chayes, "'Lower Your Sights' Is the Wrong Vision for Afghanistan," *Los Angeles Times,* March 27, 2009 (www.latimes.com/news/opinion/commentary/la-oe-chayes27-2009mar27,0,869368.story [May 28, 2009]); Testimony of Defense Secretary Robert Gates before the Senate Committee on Armed Services, January 27, 2009, p. 23; and Tellis, *Reconciling with the Taliban,* pp. 9–14.

7. DoD News Briefing with Brigadier General Larry Nicholson, July 8, 2009 (www.defenselink.mil/transcripts/transcript.aspx?transcriptid=4442 [July 10, 2009]).

8. See, for example, Richard N. Haass, *Intervention,* rev. ed. (Brookings, 1999), pp. 76–77.

9. Christopher Ward and others, *Afghanistan: Economic Incentives and Development Initiatives to Reduce Opium Production* (Washington: World Bank, February 2008), p. viii.

10. Craig Whitlock, "Diverse Sources Fund Insurgency in Afghanistan," *Washington Post,* September 27, 2009, p. A1.

11. Sometimes the words "shape" and "prepare" are placed before "clear, hold, build," but the essence of the main tasks is captured by the latter three words.

12. U.S. Army and U.S. Marine Corps, *Counterinsurgency Manual,* U.S. Army Field Manual 3-24 and Marine Corps Warfighting Publication 3-33.5 (University of Chicago Press, 2007), pp. 22–23.

13. U.S. Army, *Stability Operations,* Field Manual 3-07 (Washington: U.S. Army, October 2008) (fas.org/irp/doddir/army/fm3-07.pdf [April 1, 2009]).

14. Department of Defense, *Progress toward Security and Stability in Afghanistan, June 2009* (June 2009), p. 16 (www.defenselink.mil/pubs/pdfs/1230_June-2009Final.pdf [July 15, 2009]).

15. President Barack Obama, "Remarks by the President on a New Strategy for Afghanistan and Pakistan," White House, March 27, 2009 (www.whitehouse.gov/the_press_office/Remarks-by-the-President-on-a-New-Strategy-for-Afghanistan-and-Pakistan [May 28, 2009]).

16. Speech by Central Command Combatant Commander David Petraeus at the Center for a New American Security annual conference, "Striking the Balance," Washington, June 11, 2009 (www.cnas.org [June 15, 2009]).

17. Yochi J. Dreazen, "U.S., Allies Plan to Bolster Kandahar Force," *Wall Street Journal,* August 26, 2009 (online.wsj.com/article/SB125122932329657897.html [September 30, 2009]).

18. Petraeus speech, June 11, 2009.

19. Max Boot, Frederick W. Kagan, and Kimberly Kagan, "Yes, We Can: In the 'Graveyard' of Empires, We are Fighting a War We Can Win," *Weekly Standard,* March 23, 2009, p. 17.

20. DoD News Briefing with Col. Spiszer at the Pentagon Briefing Room via Teleconference from Afghanistan, June 23, 2009 (www.defenselink.mil/transcripts/transcript.aspx?transcriptid=4437 [June 24, 2009]).

21. General Stanley McChrystal, "COMISAF Initial Assessment," unclassified version, *Washington Post,* September 21, 2009 (www.washingtonpost.com/wp-dyn/content/article/2009/09/21/AR2009092100110_pf.html [October 1, 2009]).

22. Thom Shanker, Peter Baker, and Helene Cooper, "U.S. to Protect Populous Afghan Areas, Officials Say," *New York Times,* October 28, 2009, p. A1.

23. McChrystal, "COMISAF Initial Assessment."

24. See for example, Prime Minister Gordon Brown, "Speech on Afghanistan," International Institute for Strategic Studies, London, September 4, 2009 (www.number-10.gov.uk [October 1, 2009]).

25. McChrystal, "COMISAF Initial Assessment."

26. Petraeus speech, June 11, 2009.

27. McChrystal, "COMISAF Initial Assessment."

28. Joshua Partlow, "U.S. Gives Tour of New Afghan Detention Center," *Washington Post,* November 16, 2009, p. A10.

29. Jim Michaels, "Airstrikes in Afghanistan Drop by Almost Half," *USA Today,* September 9, 2009, p. 7.

30. Yochi J. Dreazen, "U.S. Revisits Afghan Battle Rules," *Wall Street Journal,* June 23, 2009, p. 7.

31. CBS, "Interview with General Stanley McChrystal," *60 Minutes,* September 27, 2009 (www.cbsnews.com/stories/2009/09/24/60minutes/main5335445.shtml [October 1, 2009]).

32. Eric Schmitt and Thom Shanker, "U.S. Report Finds Airstrike Errors in Afghan Deaths," *New York Times,* June 3, 2009, p. A1.

33. Petraeus speech, June 11, 2009; David Zucchino, "Fighting Afghan Information War," *Los Angeles Times,* June 11, 2009, p. 21.

34. Tom Donnelly and Tim Sullivan, "McChrystal Lite," *Weekly Standard,* November 9, 2009, pp. 16–17.

35. Petraeus speech, June 11, 2009.

36. Bruce Riedel, "How Not to Lose Afghanistan: Breaking the Taliban's Momentum," *New York Times,* January 26, 2009 (www.brookings.edu/opinions/2009/0126_afghanistan_riedel.aspx?p=1 [May 1, 2009]).

37. Eric Schmitt and Thom Shanker, "U.S. Seeks $3 Billion for Pakistani Military," *New York Times,* April 3, 2009, p. A14.

38. Interagency Policy Group, "White Paper of the Interagency Policy Group's Report on U.S. Policy toward Afghanistan and Pakistan," White House, March

27, 2009 (www.whitehouse.gov/assets/documents/Afghanistan-Pakistan_White_ Paper.pdf [May 28, 2009]).

39. O'Hanlon conversations with key NATO and Afghan leaders, Kabul and Kandahar and Helmand provinces, November 2009.

40. Tellis, *Reconciling with the Taliban?* p. 78.

41. Ministry of Finance, Islamic Republic of Afghanistan, *1388 National Budget* (Kabul, 2009) (www.budgetmof.gov.af/NationalBudget/Budget/Budget.html [June 1, 2009]).

42. Jason Campbell and Jeremy Shapiro, "The Afghanistan Index," October 8, 2009 (www.brookings.edu/foreign-policy/~/media/Files/Programs/FP/afghanistan%20index/index.pdf [October 29, 2009]).

43. Those Afghan agencies are the Independent Directorate for Local Governance and the Independent Administrative Reform and Civil Service Commission. See United Nations Development Programme/Afghanistan, "Afghanistan Sub-national Governance Programme Annual Project Report 2008," New York, 2009 (www.undp.org/WhoWeAre/UNDPinAfghanistan/Projects/Annual Report08/ASGP_AnnualReport08.pdf [May 1, 2009]), p. 4.

44. Ashraf Ghani, "A Ten-Year Framework for Afghanistan: Executing the Obama Plan . . . and Beyond," Atlantic Council, Washington, D.C., April 2009, pp. 11, 22 (www.acus.org [May 25, 2009]). Ghani is a key architect of these programs. There are now nearly 20,000 Community Development Centers, meaning that more than two-thirds of the country's villages now have them. See Ward and others, *Afghanistan: Economic Incentives and Development Initiatives to Reduce Opium Production*, p. vii.

45. Ministry of Finance, *1388 National Budget*, pp. 25–30.

46. Economic Policy and Poverty Team, South Asia Region, "Afghanistan Economic Update," Washington, September 2009, p. 1 (http://siteresources.worldbank. org/AFGHANISTANEXTN/Resources/305984-1237085035526/Afghanistan EconomicUpdateOct2009.pdf [November 19, 2009]).

47. Government of the Islamic Republic of Afghanistan, *Afghanistan National Development Strategy, 1387-1391 (2008-2013)* (Kabul, 2008), p. 50 (www.ands. gov.af/ands/final_ands/src/final/Afghanistan%20National%20Development%20 Strategy_eng.pdf [June 1, 2009]).

48. Ibid., p. 84.

49. Mary Beth Sheridan, "Kerry Says McChrystal's Troop Request Reaches 'Too Far, Too Fast,'" *Washington Post,* October 27, 2009, p. A8.

50. "Confident Karzai Looks Forward to Five More Years as Afghan Leader," *Daily Outlook Afghanistan,* August 18, 2009, p. 2 (www.outlookafghanistan.net [August 19, 2009]).

51. Much of this is drawn from Hassina Sherjan, "Talked to Death," *New York Times,* May 8, 2009 (www.nytimes.com/2009/05/08/opinion/08sherjan. html [May 28, 2009]). For related views, see Wendy Chamberlin and Marvin

Weinbaum, "The Cost of Containment," *Philadelphia Inquirer,* June 5, 2009; and Tellis, *Reconciling with the Taliban?*

52. Fotini Christia and Michael Semple, "Flipping the Taliban," *Foreign Affairs* 88, no. 4 (July/August 2009), pp. 34–45.

CHAPTER FOUR

1. Bruce Riedel, "Comparing the U.S. and Soviet Experiences in Afghanistan," *CTC Sentinel* 2, issue 5 (May 2009), p. 2 (www.ctc.usma.edu/sentinel [June 1, 2009]).

2. For a similar view, see David Kilcullen, *The Accidental Guerrilla: Fighting Small Wars in the Midst of a Big One* (Oxford University Press, 2009), p. 114.

3. Olivier Roy, *Islam and the Resistance in Afghanistan* (Cambridge University Press, 1990), pp. 171–76; Kilcullen, *The Accidental Guerrilla*, pp. 48–49; Adam Entous, "Report Finds Taliban Quadrupled in Afghanistan," *Washington Times,* October 10, 2009, p. 2; Stephen Biddle, "Assessing the Case for War in Afghanistan," Testimony before the Committee on Foreign Relations, U.S. Senate, September 16, 2009, p. 8 (www.cfr.org [September 20, 2009]).

4. Ashley J. Tellis, *Reconciling with the Taliban? Toward an Alternative Grand Strategy in Afghanistan* (Washington: Carnegie Endowment for International Peace, 2009), p. 9.

5. Jason Campbell and Michael O'Hanlon, "Iraq Index," January 29, 2007, p. 37 (www.brookings.edu/fp/saban/iraq/index20070129.pdf [June 15, 2009]).

6. International Republican Institute, "Afghanistan Public Opinion Survey: July 16–26, 2009," pp. 18, 58 (www.iri.org [August 18, 2009]).

7. Representative Donna F. Edwards, "Getting It Right on Afghanistan," *Washington Post,* May 28, 2009, p. A18.

8. Testimony of Peter Bergen, New America Foundation, before the U.S. House Committee on Oversight and Government Reform Subcommittee on National Security and Foreign Affairs, March 4, 2009.

9. Steve Coll, "What Bin Laden Sees in Hiroshima," *Washington Post,* February 6, 2005; Evan Braden Montgomery, *Nuclear Terrorism: Assessing the Threat, Developing a Response* (Washington: Center for Strategic and Budgetary Assessments, 2009), pp. 15–26.

10. Testimony of Joshua T. White, Johns Hopkins University, before the U.S. House Committee on Oversight and Government Reform Subcommittee on National Security and Foreign Affairs, March 4, 2009, p. 3.

11. DoD Directive 3000.05, November 2005 (www.defenselink.mil).

12. Headquarters, Department of the Army, *Field Manual 3-07: Stability Operations* (Department of Defense, October 2008), p. vi (www.fas.org/irp/dod-dir/army/fm3-07.pdf [October 6, 2008]).

13. National Intelligence Council, *Global Trends 2025: A Transformed World* (Washington, 2008), p. 71.

14. Tellis, *Reconciling with the Taliban?* pp. 9–11; Barbara F. Walter, "Designing Transitions from Violent Civil War," Paper 31 (La Jolla, Calif.: University of California, Institute on Global Conflict and Cooperation, 1997); Geoffrey Blainey, *The Causes of War* (New York: Free Press, 1973), p. 247.

15. See, for example, Thomas R. Pickering, Barnett Rubin, and Jamie F. Metzl, co-chairs, "Back from the Brink? A Strategy for Stabilizing Afghanistan-Pakistan" (Washington: Asia Society, April 2009), p. 7 (www.asiasociety.org/taskforces/afpak/Afghanistan-PakistanTaskForce.pdf [June 1, 2009]).

16. Eric Schmitt, "Pentagon Seeks Prison Overhaul in Afghanistan," *New York Times,* July 20, 2009, p. A1.

17. For one such suggestion in an otherwise very persuasive report, see International Crisis Group, *Afghanistan: The Need for International Resolve* (Brussels: February 2008), p. ii.

18. Statement of Lorne W. Craner, president, International Republican Institute, before the House Foreign Affairs Subcommittee on the Middle East and South Asia, October 1, 2009 (www.iri.org [October 2, 2009]).

19. Andrew F. Krepinevich Jr., *The Army and Vietnam* (Johns Hopkins University Press, 1986), pp. 3–127; U.S. Army, *Peace Operations,* Field Manual 100-23 (Department of Defense, December 1994); U.S. Army and U.S. Air Force, *Military Operations in Low Intensity Conflict,* Army Field Manual 100-20 and Air Force Field Manual 3-20 (U.S. Army, 1990); and U.S. Marine Corps, *Small Wars Manual* (Government Printing Office, 1940).

20. General David H. Petraeus, Lt. General James F. Amos, and Lt. Colonel John A. Nagl, *The U.S. Army/Marine Corps Counterinsurgency Field Manual* (University of Chicago Press, 2007), pp. 48–51.

CHAPTER FIVE

1. Fred Charles Ikle, *Every War Must End* (Columbia University Press, 1971), p. 96.

2. Andrew F. Krepinevich Jr., *The Army and Vietnam* (Johns Hopkins Press, 1986), pp. 177–214; Robert S. McNamara, *In Retrospect: The Tragedy and Lessons of Vietnam* (New York: Vintage Books, 1995), pp. 169–77, 210–12, 220–23, 233–47, 262–63, 282–93.

3. David Kilcullen, *The Accidental Guerrilla: Fighting Small Wars in the Midst of a Big One* (Oxford University Press, 2009), pp. 48–49; DoD News Briefing with Major General Mart de Kruif at the Pentagon Briefing Room via Teleconference, June 25, 2009 (www.defenselink.mil/transcripts/transcript.aspx?transcriptid=4439 [July 1, 2009]).

4. Peter Bergen, "Winning the Good War: Why Afghanistan Is not Obama's Vietnam," *Washington Monthly* (July/August 2009), p. 50.

5. David Galula, *Counterinsurgency Warfare: Theory and Practice* (New York: Praeger, 2005), pp. 70–86.

6. Jonathan J. Schroden, "Measures for Security in a Counterinsurgency," *Journal of Strategic Studies* 32, no. 5 (October 2009), pp. 715–44.

7. Andrew M. Exum and others, "Triage: The Next Twelve Months in Afghanistan and Pakistan," Center for a New American Security, Washington, June 2009, p. 25 (www.cnas.org [June 9, 2009]); Anthony H. Cordesman, "The Afghanistan Campaign: Can We Win?" Center for Strategic and International Studies, Washington, July 22, 2009, p. 23 (www.csis.org/burke/reports [July 22, 2009]).

8. Jason Campbell, Michael O'Hanlon, and Jeremy Shapiro, "Assessing Counterinsurgency and Stabilization Missions," Foreign Policy Paper 14 (Brookings, May 2009).

9. For a similar view, see David Kilcullen, *The Accidental Guerrilla,* p. 113.

10. Department of Defense, *Progress toward Security and Stability in Afghanistan,* June 2009 (Washington: June 2009), p. 31 (www.defenselink.mil/pubs/pdfs/1230_June-2009Final.pdf [July 15, 2009]).

11. DoD News Briefing with Major General Cone from Afghanistan, November 12, 2008 (www.defenselink.mil/transcripts/transcript.aspx?transcriptid=4314 [May 1, 2009]).

12. Stephen Biddle, Michael E. O'Hanlon, and Kenneth M. Pollack, "The Evolution of Iraq Strategy," in Richard N. Haass and Martin Indyk, eds., *Restoring the Balance: A Middle East Strategy for the Next President* (Brookings, 2008), p. 35.

13. Department of Defense, *Progress toward Security and Stability in Afghanistan, June 2009,* pp. 37–38.

14. Ann Scott Tyson, "'Sustained' Push Seen in Afghanistan," *Washington Post,* February 19, 2009, p. A11.

CHAPTER SIX

1. For a similar list of top concerns, see Seth G. Jones, *Counterinsurgency in Afghanistan* (Santa Monica, Calif.: RAND, 2008), pp. 16–24.

2. Obaid Younossi and others, *The Long March: Building an Afghan National Army* (Santa Monica, Calif.: RAND, 2009), p. 7.

3. Greg Jaffe and Karen DeYoung, "U.S. General Sees Afghan Army, Police Insufficient," *Washington Post,* July 11, 2009, p. A1.

4. On the importance of this, see Thomas R. Pickering, Barnett Rubin, and Jamie F. Metzl, co-chairs, "Back from the Brink? A Strategy for Stabilizing Afghanistan-Pakistan"(Washington: Asia Society, April 2009), p. 7 (www.asiasociety.org/taskforces/afpak/Afghanistan-PakistanTaskForce.pdf [June 1, 2009]).

5. Robert M. Perito, "The Interior Ministry's Role in Security Sector Reform," Special Report 223 (Washington: U.S. Institute of Peace, May 2009).

6. International Crisis Group, "Policing in Afghanistan: Still Searching for a Strategy," Asia Briefing 85 (December 18, 2008), p. 4 (www.crisisgroup.org/home/index.cfm?id=5824 [June 1, 2009]).

7. Stephen Biddle, "Seeing Baghdad, Thinking Saigon," *Foreign Affairs* 85, no. 2 (March/April 2006), pp. 2–14; Special Inspector General for Iraq Reconstruction, *Hard Lessons: The Iraq Reconstruction Experience* (Government Printing Office, 2009), p. 202.

8. Graeme Smith, "The Afghan Mission: A Toxic Triangle of Alliances Is Supplying Insurgents with Guns and Cash," *Globe and Mail (Canada),* March 21, 2009, p. A1.

9. Sarah Chayes, "Comprehensive Action Plan for Afghanistan" (Kandahar: January 2009) (www.SarahChayes.net [May 15, 2009]).

10. Anthony H. Cordesman, Adam Mausner, and David Kasten, *Winning in Afghanistan: Creating Effective Afghan Security Forces* (Washington: Center for Strategic and International Studies, May 2009), pp. 125–26.

11. Department of Defense, *Progress toward Security and Stability in Afghanistan, June 2009* (June 2009), p. 45 (www.defenselink.mil/pubs/pdfs/1230_June-2009Final.pdf [July 15, 2009]).

12. Thomas Barfield, "Culture and Custom in Nation-Building: Law in Afghanistan," *Maine Law Review* 60, no. 2 (2008), pp. 370–73.

13. Mohammad Masoom Stanekzai, "Thwarting Afghanistan's Insurgency: A Pragmatic Approach towards Peace and Reconciliation," *U.S.I.P. Special Report 212* (Washington: U.S. Institute of Peace, September 2008) (http://usip.forumone.com/resources/thwarting-afghanistan-s-insurgency-pragmatic-approach-toward-peace-and-reconciliation [June 24, 2009]).

14. David Kilcullen, *The Accidental Guerrilla: Fighting Small Wars in the Midst of a Big One* (Oxford University Press, 2009), p. 68.

15. Roland Paris, "Scaling Back Expectations in Afghanistan," CIPS Policy Brief 2 (University of Ottawa, Centre for International Policy Studies, February 2009), pp. 2–3 (www.socialsciences.uottawa.ca/cepi-cips/eng/documents/CIPS_PolicyBrief_Paris_Feb2009_001.pdf [June 1, 2009]).

16. Cordesman, Mausner, and Kasten, *Winning in Afghanistan*, pp. 138–39.

17. As General Stanley McChrystal succinctly put it, "Their past is not important. . . . I think we focus on future behavior." Quoted in Dexter Filkins, "His Long War," *New York Times Magazine,* October 18, 2009, p. 45.

18. Jones, *Counterinsurgency in Afghanistan,* p. 21.

19. Bruce Riedel, "Comparing the U.S. and Soviet Experiences in Afghanistan," *CTC Sentinel* 2, no. 5 (May 2009), p. 2 (www.ctc.usma.edu/sentinel [June 1, 2009]).

20. Dan Byman, *Deadly Connections: States That Sponsor Terrorism* (Cambridge University Press, 2005), pp. 155–97.

21. Stephen John Stedman, "Introduction," in *Ending Civil Wars: The Implementation of Peace Agreements,* edited by Stephen John Stedman, Donald Rothchild, and Elizabeth M. Cousens (Boulder, Colo.: Lynne Rienner Publishers, 2002), pp. 1–3.

22. Seth G. Jones, *In the Graveyard of Empires: America's War in Afghanistan* (New York: W. W. Norton & Co.), p. 322.

23. Ashley J. Tellis, *Reconciling with the Taliban? Toward an Alternative Grand Strategy in Afghanistan* (Washington: Carnegie Endowment for International Peace, 2009).

24. Government of the Islamic Republic of Afghanistan, *Afghanistan National Development Strategy, 1387-1391 (2008-2013)* (Kabul, 2008), pp. 155–62 (www. ands.gov.af/ands/final_ands/src/final/Afghanistan%20National%20Development %20Strategy_eng.pdf [June 1, 2009]).

25. Government of the United Kingdom, "U.K. Policy in Afghanistan and Pakistan: The Way Forward," London, April 2009, p. 20; Andrew M. Exum, Nathaniel C. Fick, Ahmed A. Humayun, and David J. Kilcullen, "Triage: The Next Twelve Months in Afghanistan and Pakistan" (Washington: Center for a New American Security, June 2009), pp. 16–17 (www.cnas.org [June 9, 2009]).

26. Central Command Combatant Commander David Petraeus, "Striking the Balance," speech at the Center for a New American Security annual conference, Washington, June 11, 2009 (www.cnas.org [June 15, 2009]).

27. Ashraf Ghani and Clare Lockhart, *Fixing Failed States: A Framework for Rebuilding a Fractured World* (Oxford University Press, 2008), pp. 217–18.

28. Oxfam, "Afghanistan: Development and Humanitarian Priorities," London, January 2008, p. 1 (www.oxfam.org/uk/resouces/policy/conflict_disasters/ downloads/afghanistan_priorities.pdf [July 1, 2008]).

29. Jane Harman and Michael O'Hanlon, "Tie Troops to Progress on Afghanistan's Corruption," *Financial Times,* September 23, 2009 (www.brookings.edu/ opinions/2009/0923_afghanistan_metrics_ohanlon.aspx [October 22, 2009]).

30. Christopher Ward and others, *Afghanistan: Economic Incentives and Development Initiatives to Reduce Opium Production* (Washington: World Bank, February 2008), pp. 40–42.

31. Peter Bergen and Sameer Lalwani, "Putting the 'I' in Aid," *New York Times,* October 2, 2009, p. 31.

32. Ashraf Ghani, "A Ten-Year Framework for Afghanistan: Executing the Obama Plan . . . and Beyond," Atlantic Council, Washington, D.C., April 2009, p. 5–6, 16 (www.acus.org [May 25, 2009]).

33. Edward Borcherdt and others, "Winning the Invisible War: An Agricultural Pilot Plan for Afghanistan," Defense and Technology Paper 46 (National Defense University, March 2008), pp. 4–5 (www.ndu.edu/ctnsp/publications. html).

34. Chayes, "Comprehensive Action Plan for Afghanistan."

35. Government of Afghanistan, *Afghanistan National Development Strategy 1387-1391*, pp. 88–94; and Department of Defense, *Progress toward Security and Stability in Afghanistan, June 2009*.

36. Ward and others, *Afghanistan: Economic Incentives and Development Initiatives to Reduce Opium*, p. 26.

37. Oxfam, "Afghanistan: Development and Humanitarian Priorities"; Riedel, *The Search for Al Qaeda* (Brookings, 2008), pp. 148–51.

38. Michael O'Hanlon and Omer Taspinar, "A Tighter Command Is Needed in Afghanistan," *Washington Times,* April 10, 2009.

39. Ghani, "A Ten-Year Framework for Afghanistan," p. 7.

40. For a different view that advocates the idea of a high commissioner with broad powers, in an important report that rightly raised warning flags about Afghanistan early in 2008, see Strategic Advisors Group, "Saving Afghanistan: An Appeal and Plan for Urgent Action," Issue Brief (Washington: Atlantic Council of the United States, March 2008), pp. 4–5.

41. Ambassador Ronald E. Neumann, "Implementation: A New Approach to Multinational Coordination in Afghanistan," Policy Analysis Brief (Muscatine, Iowa: Stanley Foundation, April 2008), p. 8.

42. Department of Defense, *Progress toward Security and Stability in Afghanistan, June 2009*, p. 48.

43. Ghani, "A Ten-Year Framework for Afghanistan," p. 18.

44. Pickering, Rubin, and Metzl, "Back from the Brink?" p. 41; Joshua Partlow and Haq Nawaz Khan, "As Violence Hurts Commerce, Pakistanis Doubt Value of U.S. Textile Bill," *Washington Post,* July 28, 2009, p. A6.

45. Subcommittee on Oversight and Investigations, Committee on Armed Services, U.S. House of Representatives, "Agency Stovepipes vs. Strategic Agility: Lessons We Need to Learn from Provincial Reconstruction Teams in Iraq and Afghanistan," U.S. Congress, April 2008, p. 51 (armedservices.house.gov/pdfs/Reports/PRT_Report.pdf [May 1, 2009]).

46. See for example, Carlos Pascual, "Building Capacity for Stabilization and Reconstruction," testimony before the House Armed Services Committee's Subcommittee on Oversight and Investigations, January 29, 2008 (www.brookings.edu/testimony/2008/0129_stabilization_pascual.aspx [June 15, 2009]).

47. Anna Husarska, "Trampled by the 'Civilian Surge,'" *Washington Post,* July 10, 2009, p. A23.

Afghanistan Index

Tracking Variables of Reconstruction and Security in Post-9/11 Afghanistan

This appendix is excerpted from the Brookings Afghanistan Index, developed and maintained over the last eighteen months by Jason Campbell, Ian Livingston, Heather Messera, and Jeremy Shapiro. The updated and complete Index is available at www.brookings.edu/afghanistanindex. Key sources for the index, itemized in the notes there, include U.S. government, NATO, and U.N. documents, icasualties.org, the Government Accountability Office, media sources, and others.

1. SECURITY INDICATORS

FIGURE 1. Estimated Number of Afghan Civilian Fatalities As a Direct Result of Fighting between Pro-Government Forces and Armed Opposition Groups (AOG), 2006–09

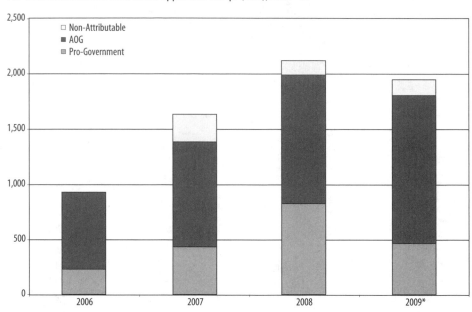

*For 2009, data is through October.

FIGURE 2. Estimated Total Afghan Civilian Fatalities by Month, 2007–Present

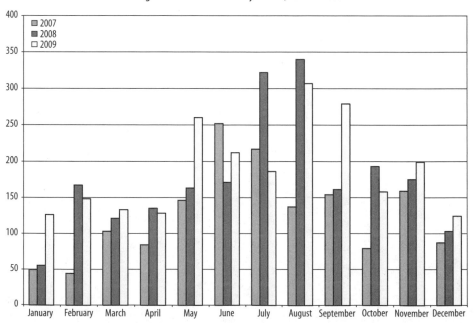

FIGURE 3. Detail of Estimated 2008 Afghan Civilian Fatalities, by Incident Type

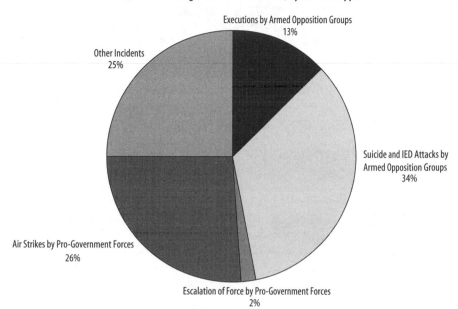

Executions by Armed Opposition Groups
13%

Other Incidents
25%

Suicide and IED Attacks by
Armed Opposition Groups
34%

Air Strikes by Pro-Government Forces
26%

Escalation of Force by Pro-Government Forces
2%

FIGURE 4. U.S. and Coalition Troop Fatalities since October 7, 2001

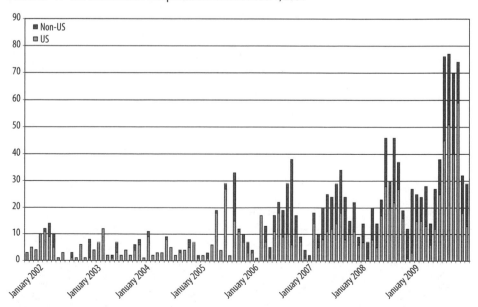

Note: December 2009 totals do not include 7 U.S. intelligence officials and 1 foreign intelligence official killed in a suicide bombing.

FIGURE 5.   Cause of Death for U.S. Troops, by Year

Year	Improvised Explosive Device	Suicide Bombs	Mortars/ RPG's/ Rockets	Landmine	Helicopter Losses	Aircraft Losses	Other Hostile Fire	Non-Hostile Causes	Total
2001	0 (0%)	0 (0%)	0 (0%)	0 (0%)	2 (16.7%)	0 (0%)	4 (33.3%)	6 (50.0%)	12
2002	5 (10.2%)	0 (0%)	1 (2.0%)	1 (2.0%)	4 (8.2%)	18 (36.7%)	12 (24.5%)	8 (16.3%)	49
2003	1 (2.1%)	0 (0%)	0 (0%)	0 (0%)	19 (39.6%)	0 (0%)	12 (25.0%)	16 (33.3%)	48
2004	12 (23.1%)	0 (0%)	1 (1.9%)	1 (1.9%)	2 (3.8%)	3 (5.8%)	10 (19.2%)	23 (44.2%)	52
2005	18 (18.2%)	0 (0%)	2 (2.0%)	5 (5.1%)	36 (36.4%)	1 (1.0%)	20 (20.2%)	17 (17.2%)	99
2006	27 (27.6%)	3 (3.1%)	1 (1.0%)	1 (1.0%)	21 (21.4%)	0 (0%)	33 (33.7%)	12 (12.2%)	98
2007	33 (28.2%)	1 (0.9%)	9 (7.7%)	1 (0.9%)	13 (11.1%)	0 (0%)	35 (29.9%)	25 21.4%)	117
2008	84 (54.2%)	4 (2.6%)	7 (4.5%)	2 (1.3%)	2 (1.3%)	0 (0%)	36 (23.2%)	20 (13.3%)	155
2009	143 (45.8%)	8 (2.6%)	21 (6.7%)	0 (0%)	13 (4.2%)	2 (0.6%)	90 (28.8%)	35 (11.2%)	312
Total	323 (34.30%)	16 (1.70%)	42 (4.50%)	11 (1.20%)	112 (11.90%)	24 (2.50%)	252 (26.80%)	162 (17.20%)	942

FIGURE 6.   American Military Fatalities by Group: October 7, 2001–December 5, 2009

Total fatalities as of December 5, 2009: 926

Category		Number of Fatalities
Gender	Male:	906
	Female:	20
Age	Younger than 22:	192
	22–24:	195
	25–30:	263
	31–35:	123
	Older than 35:	153
Component	Active:	761
	Reserve:	40
	National Guard:	125
Military service	Army:	696
	Marines:	134
	Navy:	53
	Air Force:	43
Officers/Enlisted	Officer:	133
	E5-E9:	383
	E1-E4:	410
Race/Ethnicity	American Indian or Alaska Native:	14
	Asian:	11
	Black or African American:	76
	Hispanic or Latino:	70
	Multiple races, pending or unknown:	8
	Native Hawaiian or Pacific Islander:	12
	White:	735

FIGURE 7. U.S. Troops Wounded in Action since October 30, 2001

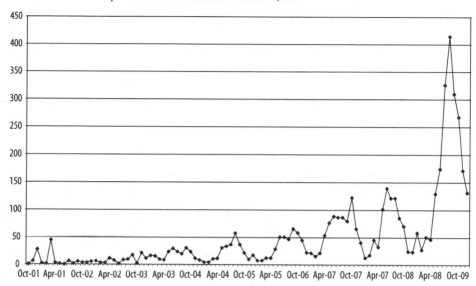

FIGURE 8. British Military Fatalities in Afghanistan since the Start of 2006

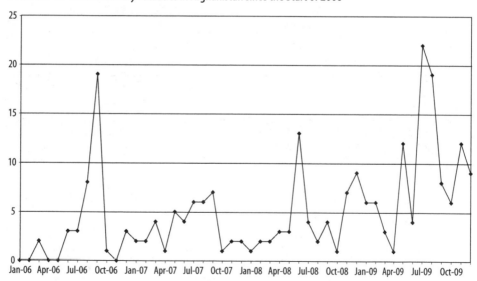

FIGURE 9. Canadian Military Fatalities in Afghanistan since the Start of 2006

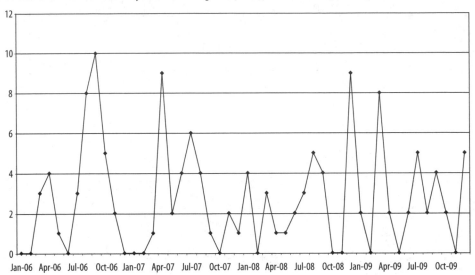

FIGURE 10. Non-U.S. Coalition Troop Fatalities by Country, October 2001–December 31, 2009

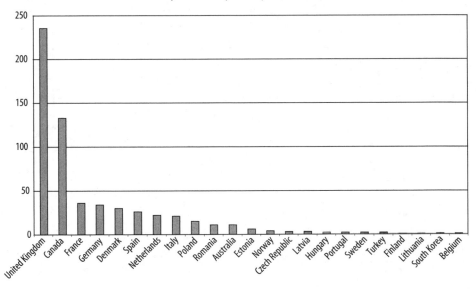

FIGURE 11. Afghan Security Force Fatalities since January 2007

Total, 2007–09: More than 3,000

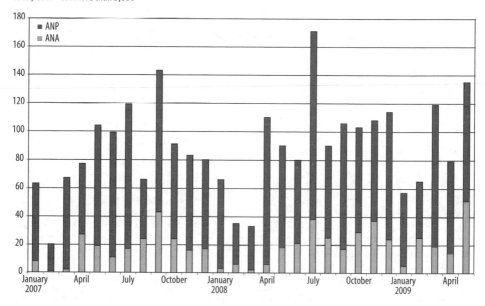

FIGURE 12. American Troops Deployed to Afghanistan

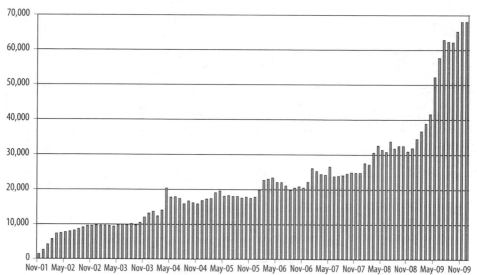

FIGURE 13. Troops Committed to NATO's International Security Assistance Forces (ISAF) by Country, as of October 22, 2009

Country	Number of Troops	Country	Number of Troops	Country	Number of Troops
Albania	250	Germany	4,365	Romania	990
Armenia	0	Greece	145	Singapore	9
Australia	1,350	Hungary	360	Slovakia	245
Azerbaijan	90	Iceland	2	Slovenia	130
Belgium	530	Ireland	7	Spain	1,000
Bosnia and Herzegovina	10	Italy	2,795	Sweden	430
Bulgaria	460	Jordan	7	The Former Yugoslav Republic	
Canada	2,830	Latvia	175	of Macedonia	165
Croatia	290	Lithuania	250	Turkey	720
Czech Republic	480	Luxembourg	8	Ukraine	10
Denmark	690	Netherlands	2,160	United Arab Emirates	25
Estonia	150	New Zealand	300	United Kingdom	9,000
Finland	165	Norway	480	United States	34,800
France	3,095	Poland	1,910		
Georgia	1	Portugal	145	Total	71,030

FIGURE 14. Size of Afghan Security Forces on Duty

Month	Ministry of Defense Forces	Ministry of Interior Forces	Total Afghan Security Forces
April 2008	57,800	79,910	137,710
October 2008	68,000	79,910	147,910
March 2009	82,780	79,910	162,690
July 2009	91,900	81,020	172,920

FIGURE 15. Size of Afghan National Army (ANA), 2003–Present

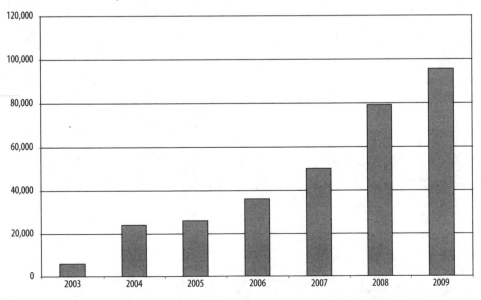

FIGURE 16. Annual Recruitment Figures for Afghan National Army (ANA)

Year	Recruits	Re-Enlistment Rate		AWOL Rate
		Soldiers	NCOs	
2003/2004	9,671			
2004/2005	15,790			
2005/2006	11,845			
2006/2007	21,287			
2007/2008	32,135	50%	56%	7%
2008/2009	~34,000	57%	63%	9%

FIGURE 17. Quality of Afghan National Army (ANA) Units and Headquarters

Units

□ Formed but not yet capable of conducting primary operational missions
□ Partially capable of conducting counterinsurgency operations at the company level with support from international forces
■ Capable of planning, executing, and sustaining counterinsurgency operations at the battalion level with international support
■ Capable of operating independently

FIGURE 18. Detailed Breakdown of Afghan Ministry of Interior Forces, as of May 2009

	Number Authorized	Number Assigned	Percent Assigned
Ministry of Interior Headquarters	5,059	4,273	84%
Uniformed Police	47,384	51,406	108%
Border Police	17,621	12,792	73%
Civil Order Police	5,365	2,462	46%
Anti-Crime	5,103	4,013	79%
Counternarcotics	2,519	3,572	142%
Fire/Medical/Training	3,149	2,388	76%
Customs Police	600	603	101%
Total	81,956	81,020	99%

FIGURE 19. Quality of Afghan National Police (ANP) Capabilities

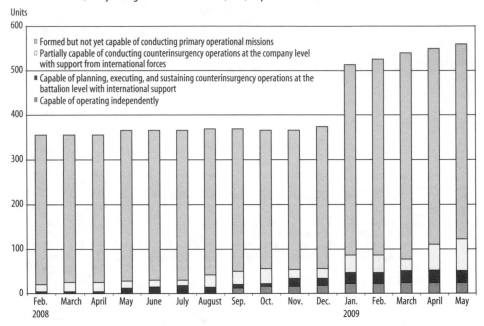

FIGURE 20. U.S. Departments of Defense and State Support to Train and Equip the Afghan Army and Police, Fiscal Years 2002–09

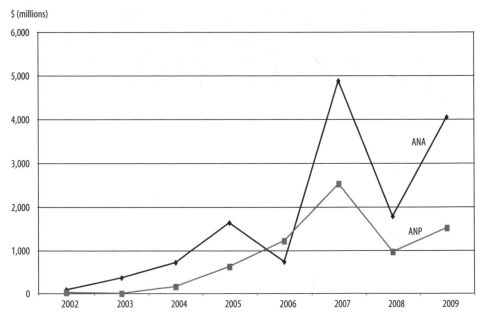

FIGURE 21. Appropriated U.S. Funding for Afghanistan by Agency, FY 2001–FY 2009
(2009 figures are partial)

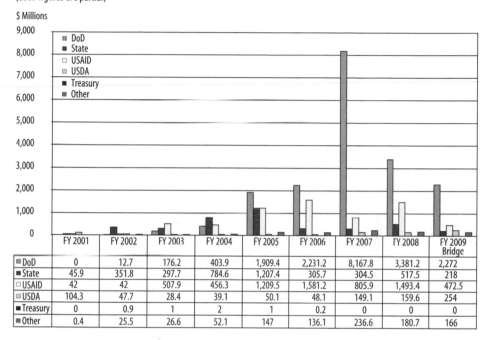

$ Millions

	FY 2001	FY 2002	FY 2003	FY 2004	FY 2005	FY 2006	FY 2007	FY 2008	FY 2009 Bridge
DoD	0	12.7	176.2	403.9	1,909.4	2,231.2	8,167.8	3,381.2	2,272
State	45.9	351.8	297.7	784.6	1,207.4	305.7	304.5	517.5	218
USAID	42	42	507.9	456.3	1,209.5	1,581.2	805.9	1,493.4	472.5
USDA	104.3	47.7	28.4	39.1	50.1	48.1	149.1	159.6	254
Treasury	0	0.9	1	2	1	0.2	0	0	0
Other	0.4	25.5	26.6	52.1	147	136.1	236.6	180.7	166

FIGURE 22. Insurgent Attacks by Month and Type, 2007–May 2009

Incidents per month

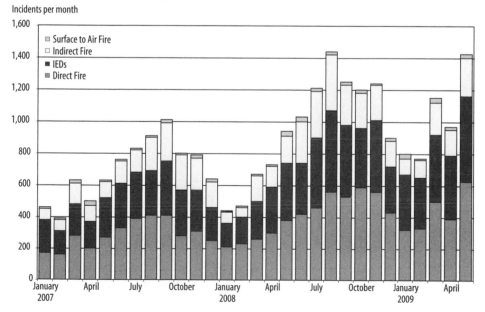

FIGURE 23. Number of Improvised Explosive Device (IED) Events by Month, 2007–May 2009

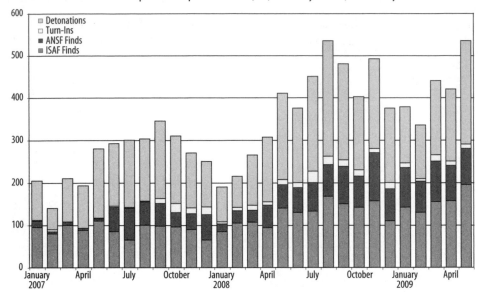

2. GOVERNANCE AND RULE OF LAW INDICATORS

FIGURE 24. Afghanistan Population and Demographic Information (2009 Estimates)

	Male	Female
Population (millions)	16.8 (51%)	15.9 (49%)

Ethnicity	Total	Percentage
Pashtun	13.7	42%
Tajik	8.8	27%
Hazara	2.9	9%
Uzbek	2.9	9%
Aimak	1.3	4%
Turkmen	1	3%
Baloch	0.7	2%
Other	1.3	4%

FIGURE 25. Size, Gender, and Ethnic Makeup of Afghanistan's Main Legislative Bodies, November 2009

	Male	Female
Number of seats	181 (73%)	68 (27%)
Total seats		249

Ethnicity	Number of Seats	Percentage
Pashtun	118	47%
Tajik	53	21%
Hazara	30	12%
Uzbek/Turkmen	25	10%
Non-Hazara Shi'a	11	4%
Arab	5	2%
Ismaili	3	1%
Pashai	2	<1%
Baluchi	1	<1%
Nuristani	1	<1%

FIGURE 26. Annual Opium Production in Afghanistan (Metric Tons) and Percentage of Global Production, 1990–2009

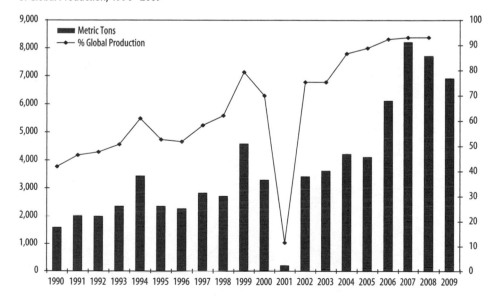

FIGURE 27. Afghanistan's Rank in Reporters without Borders' Index of Press Freedom, 2002–09

Year	Score	Rank	Number of Countries Surveyed
2009	54.2	149	175
2008	59.3	156	173
2007	56.5	142	169
2006	44.3	130	168
2005	39.2	125	167
2004	28.3	97	167
2003	40.2	134	166
2002	35.5	104	139

FIGURE 28. Afghanistan's Rank in Transparency International's Annual Corruption Perceptions Index (High Number Means High Corruption)

Year	Rank	Number of Countries Surveyed
2009	179	180
2008	176	180
2007	172 (T)	180
2006	No data	163
2005	117 (T)	159

3. ECONOMIC AND QUALITY OF LIFE INDICATORS

FIGURE 29. Annual Inflation

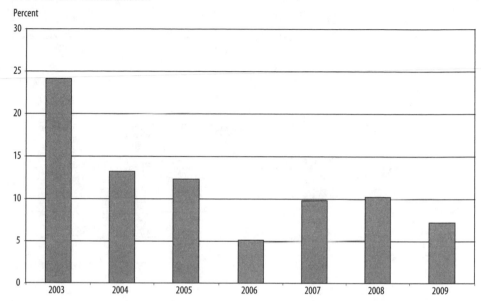

Percent

FIGURE 30. Nominal GDP (Total and Growth), 2002/2003–2009/2010

	2002/2003	2003/2004	2004/2005	2005/2006	2006/2007	2007/2008	2008/2009	2009/2010
Total ($US billions)	4.0	4.4	5.4	6.5	7.7	9.7	11.7	13.4
Growth (% change)	N/A	15.1%	8.8%	16.1%	8.2%	12.1%	3.4%	9.0%

FIGURE 31. GDP Growth and Sector Contributions to Growth, 2003–07

Percent

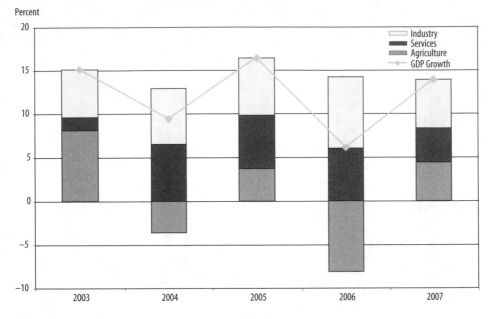

FIGURE 32. Annual Production of Major Agricultural Produce, by Planting Season

000's Metric Tons

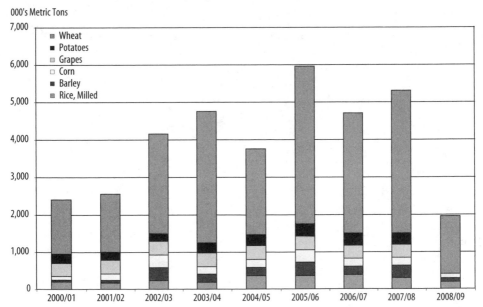

F I G U R E 3 3 . Comparison of Electricity Supply Sources and Capacity: 1979, 2002 and 2007

Year	Hydro (MW)	Thermal (MW)	Imported (MW)	Other (MW)	Total Supply (MW)
1979	259	137	0	0	396
2002	16	16	87	0	243
2007	90	90	167	133	652

F I G U R E 3 4 . Estimated Number of Telephone Users in Afghanistan by Year, 2002–09

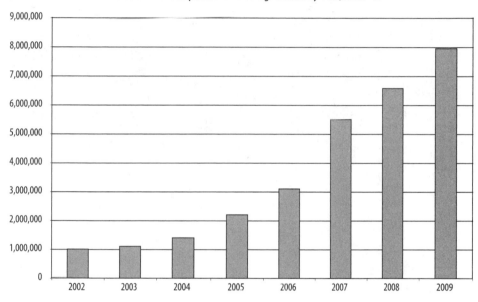

F I G U R E 3 5 . Estimated Percentage of Afghans with Access to Water/Sanitation Facilities

Access to safe drinking water	23%
Access to adequate sanitation	12%

FIGURE 36. Estimated Number of Children in School, 2002–09

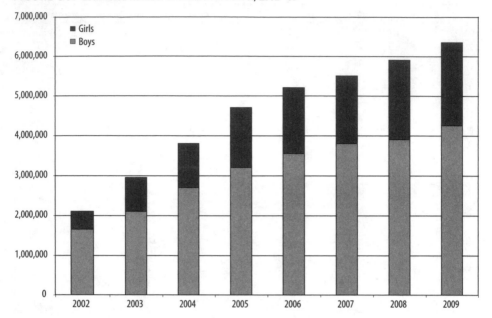

FIGURE 37. Foreign Aid Pledged, Committed and Disbursed, 2002–11 ($ Millions)

Donor	Aid Disbursed 2002–08	Aid Committed but not Disbursed 2002–08	Aid Pledged through 2009 for 2002–11 (not Committed/Disbursed)
US/USAID	5,022.90	5,377.00	12,389.10
Japan/JICA	1,393.50	16.9	0
United Kingdom	1,266.30	188.9	0
European Commission	1,074.10	646.7	19.2
World Bank	852.7	750.7	1,023.80
Germany	767.8	458.2	0
Canada	730.7	48.1	338.9
Asian Development Bank	547.8	1,009.70	183.1
Italy	424.4	0	0
Netherlands	407.1	85.5	0
Norway	277	122.3	0
Sweden	217.3	41.2	11.3
Iran	213.9	13.9	126.2
ECHO*	207.7	2.2	58.3
India	204.3	650.9	86.9
Australia	194.8	0	27.6
UN Agencies	171	0	0
Denmark	152.8	59.9	63
Russian Federation	139	0	0
Aga Khan	119.3	0	0
France	79.9	29.5	0
Saudi Arabia	76.9	30	113.1
Finland	46.1	29.9	14
Switzerland	51.6	44	0
China	41	20.4	84.2
Spain	25.6	37.2	190.5
Turkey	20.8	22.8	46.4
Total	14,726.30	9,685.90	14,775.60

FIGURE 38.   Annual Value of Imports and Exports, with Top Trade Partners, 2002–06 ($ Millions)

	2002	2003	2004	2005	2006
Exports (Total)	87	210	185	239	274
Pakistan	28	28	45	48	57
India	17	32	39	51	59
United States	4	57	23	62	42
Imports (Total)	1,034	1,608	1,971	3,002	3,633
Pakistan	245	449	511	1,172	1,375
United States	88	67	173	288	459
Germany	57	103	130	167	275
India	57	137	170	158	186
Republic of Korea	141	137	85	66	77
Turkmenistan	31	81	107	122	143
Japan	92	114	73	84	74

FIGURE 39.   Healthcare Metrics

Year	% People Living In Districts Where Basic Package of Health Care (BPHC) Is Available
2003	9%
2005	77%
2006	82%

4. POLLING AND PUBLIC OPINION

FIGURE 40. Do You Think Afghanistan Is Moving in the Right Direction or the Wrong Direction? (International Republican Institute Poll)

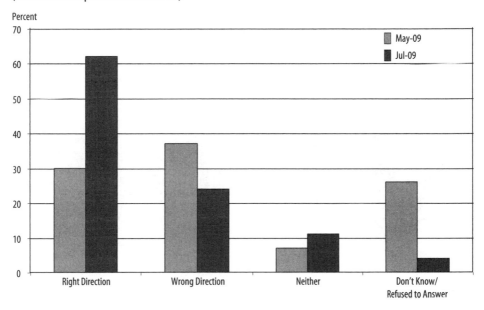

FIGURE 41. How Would You Describe the Political and Security Situation in the Region? (IRI Poll)

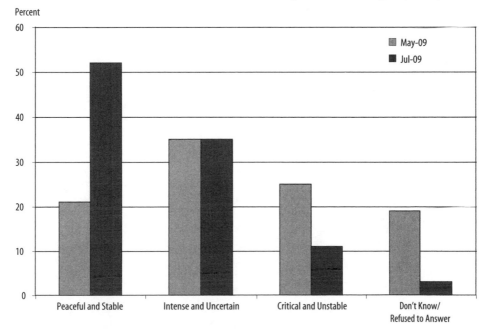

FIGURE 42. Is Afghanistan More Stable Today than it Was One Year Ago? (IRI Poll)

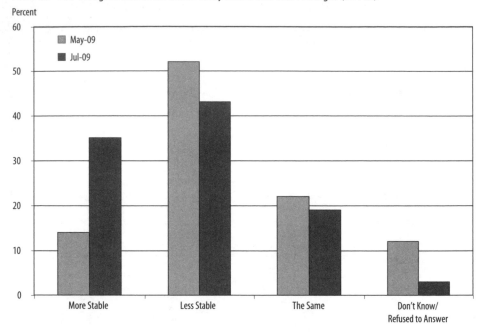

FIGURE 43. Did You Have More Personal Freedom during or after Taliban Rule? (IRI Poll)

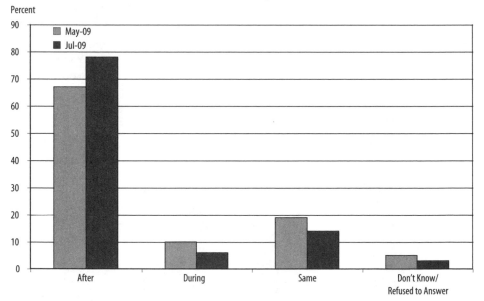

FIGURE 44. How Is Your family's Economic Situation Compared to Five Years Ago? (IRI Poll)

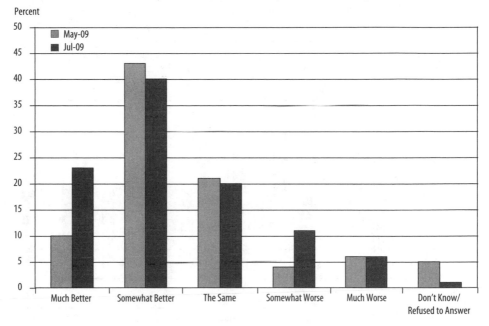

FIGURE 45. In the Next Year, Do You Think the Economy in Afghanistan Will Get Better, Get Worse or Stay the Same? (IRI Poll)

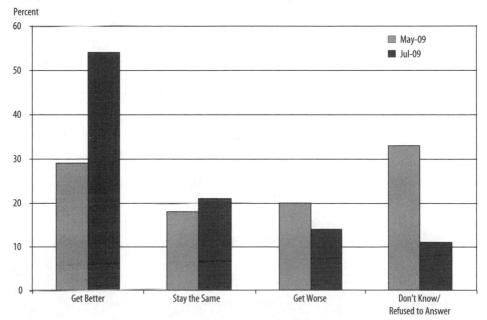

FIGURE 46. Do You Have a Favorable or Unfavorable Opinion of the Following Groups, Organizations, or Countries? (IRI Poll, July 2009)

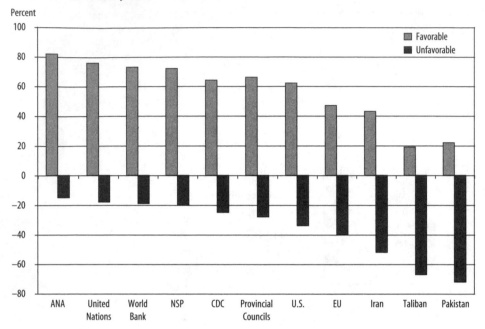

FIGURE 47. Generally Speaking, Do You Think Things in Afghanistan Today Are Going in the Right Direction, or Do You Think They Are Going in the Wrong Direction? (ABC/BBC/ARD Poll, Feb. 2009 and Before)

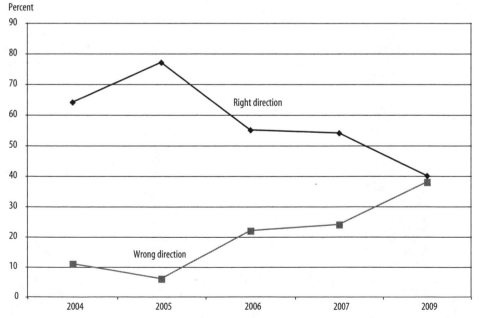

FIGURE 48. Performance Ratings for Various Entities (ABC/BBC/ARD Poll, Feb. 2009 and Before)

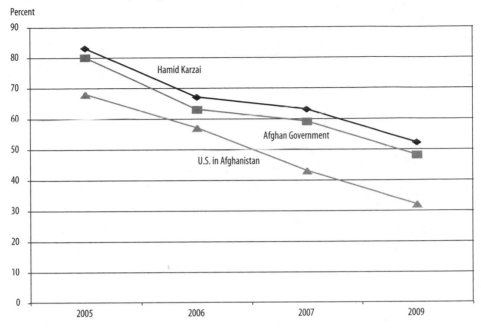

FIGURE 49. Is Your Opinion of the Taliban Very Favorable, Somewhat Favorable, Somewhat Unfavorable or Very Unfavorable? (ABC/BBC/ARD Poll, Feb. 2009 and Before)

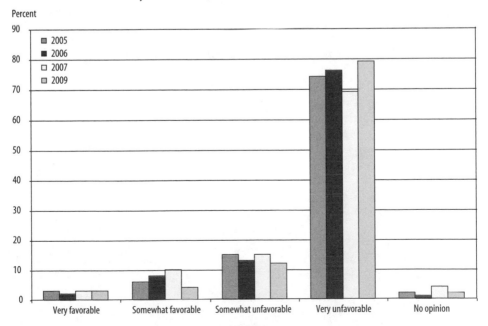

FIGURE 50. Who Would You Rather Have Ruling Afghanistan Today? (ABC/BBC/ARD Poll, Feb. 2009 and Before)

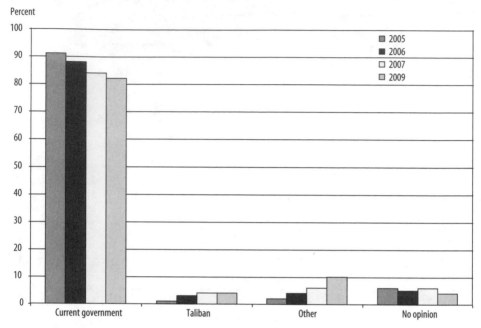

FIGURE 51. Which of the Following Do You Think Poses the Biggest Danger in Afghanistan? (ABC/BBC/ARD Poll, Feb. 2009 and Before)

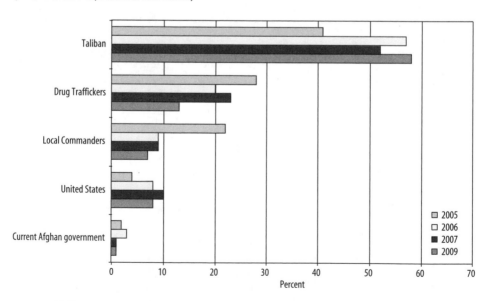

FIGURE 52.   How Much of a Problem Is the Issue of Corruption among Government Officials or the Police in Your Area of Afghanistan? (ABC/BBC/ARD Poll, Feb. 2009 and Before)

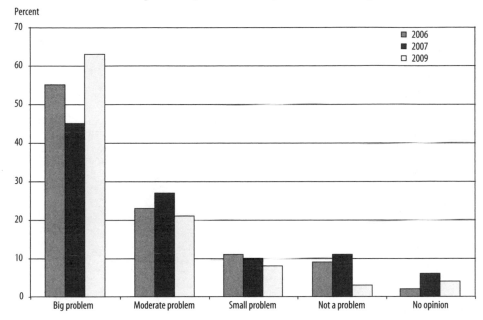

Index